THE SEARCH FOR EQUITY
IN SCHOOL FINANCE

A Rand Educational Policy Study

THE SEARCH FOR EQUITY IN SCHOOL FINANCE

STEPHEN J. CARROLL
and
ROLLA EDWARD PARK

BALLINGER PUBLISHING COMPANY
Cambridge, Massachusetts
A Subsidiary of Harper & Row, Publishers, Inc.

International Standard Book Number: 0–88410–840–6

Library of Congress Catalog Card Number: 82–11510

Printed in the United States of America

Library of Congress Cataloging in Publication Data

Carroll, Stephen J., 1940–
    The search for equity in school finance.

    (A Rand educational policy study)
    Includes bibliographical references and index.
    1. Education—United States—Finance. I. Park,
Rolla Edward. II. Title. III. Series.
LB2825.C316 1982   379.1′22′0973   82–11510
ISBN 0–88410–840–6

CONTENTS

List of Tables   ix

Preface   xiii

Chapter 1
Introduction   1
Study Approach   5
Outline of the Study   7

Chapter 2
Principal Findings   9
Reform Plans in the Sample States   9
The Effects of Reform in California   11
The Effects of Reform in Florida   12
The Effects of Reform in Kansas   13
The Effects of Reform in Michigan   14
The Effects of Reform in New Mexico   15
Conclusions   15

Chapter 3
Variables and Measures   17
Background   17
Reform Themes   19

Fiscal Outcomes   20
Fiscal Neutrality   27
Variables of Interest   29
Weights   31
Measures of Distributional Equality   32
Measures of Fiscal Neutrality   34
Winners and Losers   37
Data   38

Chapter 4
The Effects of Reform in California   41

School Finance in California   41
Data and Definitions   46
Elementary School Districts   47
  The Distribution of Revenues, Instructional
    Expenditures, and Adjusted Tax Rates   47
  Wealth, Income, and Tax Neutrality   52
  Winners and Losers   54
High School Districts   55
  The Distribution of Revenues, Instructional
    Expenditures, and Adjusted Tax Rates   55
  Wealth, Income, and Tax Neutrality   61
  Winners and Losers   63
Unified School Districts   66
  The Distribution of Revenues, Instructional
    Expenditures, and Adjusted Tax Rates   66
  Wealth, Income, and Tax Neutrality   70
  Winners and Losers   72
Summary and Conclusions   73

Chapter 5
The Effects of Reform in Florida   79

School Finance in Florida   79
Data and Definitions   81
The Effect of Pupil Weights in Florida   82
The Distribution of Revenues, Instructional Expenditures,
  and Adjusted Tax Rates   83
Wealth, Income, and Tax Neutrality   85

Winners and Losers   88
Summary and Conclusions   90

Chapter 6
The Effects of Reform in Kansas   93

School Finance in Kansas   93
Data and Definitions   97
Districts with ADM below 400   99
   The Distribution of Revenues, Instructional Expenditures,
     and Adjusted Tax Rates   99
   Wealth, Income, and Tax Neutrality   102
   Winners and Losers   104
Districts with ADM between 400 and 1,299   106
   The Distribution of Revenues, Instructional Expenditures,
     and Adjusted Tax Rates   106
   Wealth, Income, and Tax Neutrality   109
   Winners and Losers   112
Districts with ADM 1,300 and Above   114
   The Distribution of Revenues, Instructional Expenditures,
     and Adjusted Tax Rates   114
   Wealth, Income, and Tax Neutrality   117
   Winners and Losers   117
Summary and Conclusions   119

Chapter 7
The Effects of Reform in Michigan   123

School Finance in Michigan   123
Data and Definitions   125
The Distribution of Revenues and Adjusted Tax Rates   127
Wealth, Income, and Tax Neutrality   129
Winners and Losers   131
Summary and Conclusions   131

Chapter 8
The Effects of Reform in New Mexico   135

School Finance in New Mexico   135
Data and Definitions   139

The Distribution of Revenues, Instructional Expenditures,
    and Adjusted Tax Rates   140
Wealth, Income, and Tax Neutrality   143
Winners and Losers   145
Summary and Conclusions   147

Chapter 9
Interstate Comparisons and Conclusions   151

The Effects of Reform on Revenues, Spending, and
    Tax Rates   151
The Effects of Reform on Distributional Equality   155
The Effects of Reform on Fiscal Neutrality   157
Winners and Losers   162
Conclusions   167
Why Reform Did Not Achieve More   169

References   175

Rand Educational Policy Studies   177

Index   179

About the Authors   185

LIST OF TABLES

4–1 Summary Data on California Elementary,
     High School, and Unified Districts   44
4–2 Numbers of California Districts and Students   47
4–3 Measures of the Distribution of Revenues,
     Instructional Expenditures, and Adjusted Tax
     Rates: California Elementary Districts, 1970–76   48
4–4 Elasticity of Revenues, Instructional Expenditures,
     and Adjusted Tax Rates with Respect to Adjusted
     Wealth, Household Income, and Adjusted Tax Rates:
     California Elementary Districts, 1970–76   53
4–5 Distribution of Revenues, Instructional Expenditures,
     and Adjusted Tax Rates by District Characteristic:
     California Elementary Districts, 1970–76   56
4–6 Measures of the Distribution of Revenues, Instructional
     Expenditures, and Adjusted Tax Rates: California
     High School Districts, 1970–76   58
4–7 Elasticity of Revenues, Instructional Expenditures,
     and Adjusted Tax Rates with Respect to Adjusted
     Wealth, Household Income, and Adjusted Tax Rates:
     California High School Districts, 1970–76   62
4–8 Distribution of Revenues, Instructional Expenditures,
     and Adjusted Tax Rates by District Characteristic:
     California High School Districts, 1970–76   64

4–9   Measures of the Distribution of Revenues, Instructional
       Expenditures, and Adjusted Tax Rates: California
       Unified Districts, 1970–76   68
4–10   Elasticity of Revenues, Instructional Expenditures,
       and Adjusted Tax Rates with Respect to Adjusted
       Wealth, Household Income, and Adjusted Tax Rates:
       California Unified Districts, 1970–76   71
4–11   Distribution of Revenues, Instructional Expenditures,
       and Adjusted Tax Rates by District Characteristic:
       California Unified Districts, 1970–76   74
5–1   Summary of Florida School Districts   81
5–2   Measures of the Distribution of Revenues,
       Instructional Expenditures, and Adjusted Tax Rates:
       Florida Districts, 1972 and 1975   84
5–3   Elasticity of Revenues, Instructional Expenditures,
       and Adjusted Tax Rates with Respect to Adjusted
       Wealth, Household Income, and Adjusted Tax Rates:
       Florida Districts, 1972 and 1975   86
5–4   Distribution of Revenues, Instructional Expenditures,
       and Adjusted Tax Rates by District Characteristic:
       Florida Districts, 1972 and 1975   89
6–1   Summary of Kansas School Districts   97
6–2   Available Finance and Census Data on Kansas
       Districts and Students, by Enrollment Level,
       1972–73 through 1974–75   98
6–3   Measures of the Distribution of Revenues,
       Instructional Expenditures, and Adjusted Tax Rates:
       Kansas Districts with ADM below 400, 1972–74   100
6–4   Elasticity of Revenues, Instructional Expenditures,
       and Adjusted Tax Rates with Respect to Adjusted
       Wealth, Household Income, and Adjusted Tax Rates:
       Kansas Districts with ADM below 400, 1972–74   103
6–5   Distribution of Revenues, Instructional Expenditures,
       and Adjusted Tax Rates by District Characteristic:
       Kansas Districts with ADM below 400, 1972–74   105
6–6   Measures of the Distribution of Revenues, Instructional
       Expenditures, and Adjusted Tax Rates: Kansas
       Districts with ADM between 400 and 1,299,
       1972–74   107
6–7   Elasticity of Revenues, Instructional Expenditures,
       and Adjusted Tax Rates with Respect to Adjusted

Wealth, Household Income, and Adjusted Tax Rates: Kansas Districts with ADM between 400 and 1,299, 1972–74   110

6–8   Distribution of Revenues, Instructional Expenditures, and Adjusted Tax Rates by District Characteristic: Kansas Districts with ADM between 400 and 1,299, 1972–74   113

6–9   Measures of the Distribution of Revenues, Instructional Expenditures, and Adjusted Tax Rates: Kansas Districts with ADM 1,300 and above, 1972–74   115

6–10   Elasticity of Revenues, Instructional Expenditures, and Adjusted Tax Rates with Respect to Adjusted Wealth, Household Income, and Adjusted Tax Rates: Kansas Districts with ADM 1,300 and above, 1972–74   118

6–11   Distribution of Revenues, Instructional Expenditures, and Adjusted Tax Rates by District Characteristic: Kansas Districts with ADM 1,300 and above, 1972–74   120

7–1   Summary of Michigan School Districts   126

7–2   Available Finance and Census Data on Michigan K–12 Districts and Students, 1971–72 through 1975–76   127

7–3   Measures of the Distribution of Revenues, Instructional Expenditures, and Adjusted Tax Rates: Michigan Districts, 1971–75   128

7–4   Elasticity of Revenues, Instructional Expenditures, and Adjusted Tax Rates with Respect to Adjusted Wealth, Household Income, and Adjusted Tax Rates: Michigan Districts, 1971–75   130

7–5   Distribution of Revenues, Instructional Expenditures, and Adjusted Tax Rates by District Characteristic: Michigan Districts, 1971–75   132

8–1   Summary of New Mexico Districts   136

8–2   Measures of the Distribution of Revenues, Instructional Expenditures, and Adjusted Tax Rates: New Mexico Districts, 1972–75   141

8–3   Elasticity of Revenues, Instructional Expenditures, and Adjusted Tax Rates with Respect to Adjusted Wealth, Household Income, and Adjusted Tax Rates: New Mexico Districts, 1972–75   144

8–4   Distribution of Revenues, Instructional Expenditures, and Adjusted Tax Rates by District Characteristic: New Mexico Districts, 1972–75   146

9–1   Revenues per Pupil, Instructional Expenditures
       per Pupil, and Adjusted Tax Rates   152
9–2   Coefficients of Variation for Revenues, Instructional
       Expenditures, and Adjusted Tax Rates   154
9–3   Elasticity of Revenues per Pupil and Instructional
       Expenditures per Pupil with Respect to Adjusted
       Wealth per Pupil   159
9–4   Elasticity of Revenues per Pupil and Instructional
       Expenditures per Pupil with Respect to Household
       Income per Pupil   160
9–5   Elasticity of Revenues per Pupil and Instructional
       Expenditures per Pupil with Respect to Adjusted
       Tax Rates   162
9–6   Ratios of Average Per-Pupil Revenues in Districts
       below the Median on a District Characteristic to
       Average Per-Pupil Revenues in Districts above the
       Median on the Characteristic   163
9–7   Ratios of Average Per-Pupil Instructional Expenditures
       in Districts below the Median on a District Characteristic
       to Average Per-Pupil Instructional Expenditures in
       Districts above the Median on the Characteristic   164
9–8   Ratios of Average Adjusted Tax Rates in Districts
       below the Median on a District Characteristic to
       Average Adjusted Tax Rates in Districts above the
       Median on the Characteristic   165

PREFACE

The Rand Corporation has analyzed recent school finance reforms in five states: California, Florida, Kansas, Michigan, and New Mexico. The main objective of the study is to describe the pre-reform and post-reform outcomes in each state, compare the outcomes in each state, and compare the outcomes among the states. For each state the descriptive analysis examines pre- and post-reform distributions of revenues, expenditures, and tax rates; the degree to which reform has been accompanied by an increase in intrastate fiscal neutrality; and the kinds of districts that have benefited most and least from reform. The overall purpose is to provide information for officials in states that have yet to undertake or to complete reform, and for federal officials with responsibilities in school finance.

The research was performed with support from the National Institute of Education. The Rand Corporation supported preparation of this book with corporate funds. We are indebted to the National Conference of State Legislatures for data on the school districts of Florida and Kansas, to James Phelps, associate superintendent for research and administration, Michigan State Department of Education, for data on Michigan's school districts, and to Robert Brischetto of the Intercultural Development Research Association for data on New Mexico's school districts. We received helpful comments and suggestions from Dennis Doyle (National Institute of Education), James Fox (Office of the Assistant Secretary for Education), James Kelly

(The Ford Foundation), David Mandel (National Institute of Education), and Allen Odden (Education Commission of the States), and from Rand colleagues Arthur Alexander, Paul Hill, David Lyon, Dan Weiler, and Arthur Wise. We are particularly indebted to Stephen Barro, who formulated much of the original plan for this study while at Rand, and participated in the early phases of the work.

Millicent Cox of Rand obtained the data employed in this study and performed the complex tasks required to combine information from a variety of sources into an accessible data base for each state. She also developed detailed descriptions of each state's pre- and post-reform school finance plans; the summary descriptions that appear at the beginning of each state's chapter were derived from her work. William Lisowski of Rand performed the vast number of computations required to develop the substantial measures discussed in the text.

We were not always able to follow the advice we received; any errors of commission or omission are our sole responsibility.

Stephen J. Carroll
Rolla Edward Park

1 INTRODUCTION

Equality of educational opportunity, as defined by expenditures per child, was a public policy issue throughout the 1970s and still remains unresolved. For years to come, disputes over the equity of state school finance systems will claim the energies of federal, state, and local government officials and legislators, and the judiciary, researchers, citizens' advocacy groups, taxpayers, and parents. The policies that emerge from these debates will determine how the largest single item in state and local government finance (more than $80 billion in 1978) is distributed among the nation's local school systems and how the burden of supporting the schools is distributed among taxpayers. Issues that transcend money are ultimately involved. Education is crucial to the perpetuation of a society, it being the primary means by which society inculcates its values in its citizenry; and education is important to the future social and economic well-being of the individual pupil.

Local government has traditionally provided the bulk of local school districts' revenues. In 1970, school districts obtained about 52 percent of their revenues locally, mostly from property taxes. States provided about 40 percent, and federal sources 8 percent. Many people believed that the heavy reliance on property taxes was inequitable. A school district that enjoyed a high property tax base per pupil could raise abundant money with a low property tax rate. A district with a low per pupil tax base could raise less money even if it levied a high

1

rate; it thereby would suffer the dual disadvantage of a high tax rate and limited funds for school spending. In other words, where a family lived largely determined the quality of its children's education—insofar as quality can be measured by expenditures per pupil.

Growing recognition of this problem gave birth to a reform movement that spread across the country in the early 1970s. Its first major victory came in 1971 when the California supreme court, in its landmark *Serrano* v. *Priest* decision, found the state's school finance system in violation of both the state and federal constitutions: The California "funding scheme invidiously discriminates against the poor because it makes the quality of a child's education a function of the wealth of his parents and neighbors." Because most other states' school finance systems resemble California's, the *Serrano* victory touched off a race for reform. Some fifty-two similar actions were promptly filed in thirty-one states. With few exceptions, the courts agreed with the *Serrano* reasoning, and one state after another found its school finance system struck down.[1] At the same time, numerous states set out to modify their systems through the legislative process. By 1977, at least twenty-five states (as many as thirty-one by some counts) had overhauled their financial structures to provide greater equity in education funding.

The reform debate continues, both in states that have not modified their finance systems and in those that have.[2] The former are subject to political and, sometimes, judicial pressure; nor have pressures for change eased in the latter. Several of the reforms undertaken during the 1970s are the focus of continuing controversy over whether they have gone too far, or not far enough, or represent the wrong approach to equal educational opportunity, or are no longer appropriate to an era of fiscal limits. California's experience is illustrative.

California reformed its school finance system in 1973, only to have its new plan struck down three years later when the state's supreme court found it an insufficient response to its *Serrano* mandate. The leg-

---

[1] In 1973, the U.S. Supreme Court, in *Rodriguez* v. *San Antonio [Texas] Board of Education*, found that the Texas system—though blatantly inequitable—was a "reasonable" means for furthering legitimate state objectives and was not in violation of the federal constitution. Other states' constitutional guarantees, however, provided sufficient grounds for successful legal challenges to their finance systems.

[2] The word "reform" has normative connotations; it suggests that something is wrong and that change will improve or correct the situation. While we do not wish to imply that all recent changes in state school financing systems were necessarily for the better, we follow contemporary usage in the school finance community and refer to these changes as "reforms."

islature then shaped a second reform plan, which partially took effect in 1977. Most of its provisions, however, became irrelevant in the wake of Proposition 13, a constitutional limit on property tax rates approved by the voters in June 1978. The reform debate was rekindled as the legislature developed a temporary finance plan for the 1978 school year, and then again as yet another school finance formula—the fourth of the decade—was fashioned in the spring of 1979. Within a month after its enactment, the Los Angeles *Times* reported (August 14, 1979) that attorney John McDermott, who won the *Serrano* decision, would ask the California supreme court to overturn the new plan because it did not sufficiently equalize spending across the state's school districts. And so the debate goes on.

Although the other reform states have thus far escaped so extreme a series of marches and countermarches, the question of whether they have made the "right" decisions in formulating their reforms remains at issue. The issue is further complicated by the recent entrance of the federal government into the arena. The impact aid program [Public Law (PL) 874] now permits states that have "adequate" school finance equalization programs to count a district's impact aid grant as a local revenue; the states have received federal grants to help them plan for equalization; the Congress has held hearings on direct federal incentives to states that reformed their systems and has mandated a massive three-year analysis of the financing of elementary and secondary education. States are thus becoming subject to a whole new set of pressures to reform (or rereform) their systems.

The question of what constitutes an equitable state school finance system is now, more than ever, an important public policy concern. The exasperated citizen may reasonably inquire, Why is that question so hard to answer? Why don't states simply set up an equitable system and be done with it? The reply is that at least three sets of factors stand in the way: differences in values and objectives, political realities, and information gaps.

Parties to the school finance debate approach the issue from different perspectives and with different objectives in mind, and have championed dissimilar, and often mutually exclusive, concepts of equity. Reform advocates may completely agree that a state's finance system needs to be modified, and as completely disagree on what an equitable reform should consist of. And while the reformers are arguing, other people may quietly join the fray to promote goals not directly related to equity. At least some of the debates seem to be less concerned with how reform should affect the distribution of funds among districts than with what else should be done when a state revamps its finance system.

Reform necessarily implies a redistribution of funds, or of tax burdens, or both, among districts. At least some districts are thus threatened with lower revenues or heavier tax burdens, or both. Not surprisingly, they and their representatives often oppose reform efforts or attempt to co-opt them by advocating reforms that touch them the least. Similarly, interest groups and their representatives may back the types of reforms that promise the most revenues or the greatest tax relief to the districts where their constituents are concentrated. Even the "have-not" districts, who stand to gain from reform, disagree over what is the most appropriate reform. Because their situations differ, any particular type of reform will benefit some more than others.

Finally, it is difficult to foresee the outcomes of any reform plan. Value judgments and political realities aside, people often disagree about the likely effects of various reform proposals, nor is the track record thus far very illuminating. The reforms that states have undertaken differ in degree and kind, but no consistent body of information has been compiled either on how well reforms have worked in the individual states or on the relative effects of various approaches to reform.

This book assesses the outcomes of reform in five states—California, Florida, Kansas, Michigan, and New Mexico—whose new financing laws represent the major approaches to reform in the post-*Serrano* era. We describe the extent to which each state's reform affected the levels and distributions of revenues, instructional expenditures, and local educational property tax rates. We also investigate the degree to which school districts' revenues, instructional expenditures, and local property tax rates are associated with their fiscal capacities of efforts before and after reform in each state. We describe the ways in which these elements have been redistributed among districts according to their differing characteristics. Finally, we speculate on why each state's reform yielded the observed results.

This study does not pretend to be an evaluation of school finance reform, or of any particular reform plan, there being no generally agreed-upon criteria for measuring the outcomes of reform. Nor do we suggest the legislators who enacted these plans, or the governors who signed them into law, had any particular set of objectives in mind. We do not imply, for example, that they were specifically concerned with levels or distributions of revenues, or instructional expenditures, or tax rates, or the degree to which tax rates are associated with fiscal capacities or efforts, or with any other goals that the reform plan might have promoted. But regardless of what the plans' developers and sup-porters—or, for that matter, opponents—wanted to accomplish or thought they would achieve, the plans do affect these outcomes; and the direction and magnitude of the outcomes are of interest to policymakers concerned with school finance and, more generally, to the citizens who pay the costs and reap the benefits of reform. Our ob-jective is to provide information on how various distributions and re-lationships changed with reform in each state. It is for the reader to judge whether those changes were for the better or for the worse, whether more—or less—needs to be done in any state, and, in any event, whether reform has been "worth the effort."

STUDY APPROACH

Most (but not all) reform proposals embrace one or the other of two basic themes, or some compromise between them. The first is equali-zation of fiscal outcomes among a state's school districts. This theme emerges from the egalitarian principle that all students and all tax-payers in a state should be treated alike: No student (or taxpayer) should enjoy a more expensive education (or lower tax burden) than that afforded to others. In that view, the prereform systems were in-equitable because they allowed students and taxpayers in wealthy dis-tricts (high per-pupil tax base) to obtain a more expensive education while enjoying a lower tax burden.

The second theme is equalization of fiscal opportunities among school districts. This theme reflects a concern for local control of the schools or, more generally, for local public agencies. The prereform plans were inequitable, according to this view, because low-wealth communities had to levy much higher tax rates to achieve the same level of spending as high-wealth communities. The problem went deeper than sheer disparity in school spending: The low-wealth dis-tricts had less ability to raise school revenues than did high-wealth communities. It was therefore argued that a state's school finance sys-tem should be fiscally neutral, in the sense that any district could ob-tain the same level of funding as any other district, provided only that it put forth the same tax effort.

The two main themes, then, direct our interest toward the effects of each state's reform on the distributions of fiscal outcomes among its school districts, and on the relationships between those outcomes and the districts' fiscal capacities or efforts. Even casual observation confirms that many interested parties evaluate reforms by their impact on specific kinds of communities or people (e.g., central cities, low income people); to accommodate readers' particular interests, we therefore examine how various types of districts fared under each state's reform.

We obtained data from state sources on district revenues, expenditures, tax rates, wealth, and numbers of pupils. Data on the characteristics of the community served by a school district were obtained from the 1970 census, fifth count, compiled to 1974 school district boundaries. Our data are for the following years:

State	Year Reform Introduced	Years for Which Data Were Available
California	1973–74	1970–71 through 1976–77
Florida	1973–74	1972–73, 1975–76
Kansas	1973–74	1972–73 through 1974–75
Michigan	1973–74	1971–72 through 1975–76
New Mexico	1974–75	1972–73 through 1975–76

To provide useful information for comparing our results with those of other studies, we examined the effects of reform on as many notions of fiscal outcomes and opportunities as we could, given the resources and data available to us. Specifically, we consider five measures of current revenues per pupil, and local property taxes. We compare the prereform and postreform distributions of each variable; the relationships between each variable and wealth per pupil, household income, and, for the first six variables, the tax rate; and the distributions of each variable among districts distinguished by their size and by their percentages of urban, minority, and poverty population.

In each case we use an array of statistical measures to evaluate distributional disparities and degrees of relationship. Here again, we seek to serve the information needs of people with different views of how distributions of fiscal outcomes or of fiscal opportunities should be summarized. The discussion concentrates on the results obtained using the pupil as the unit of analysis. Parallel results, using the district as the unit of analysis, are provided in Carroll (1979).

OUTLINE OF THE STUDY

For the convenience of readers primarily interested in the effects of a particular state's reform, Chapter 2 briefly summarizes our principal findings and conclusions for each of the five states. Chapter 3 describes the fiscal outcomes and opportunities we examined and the statistical measures we employed to assess prereform and postreform distributions and relationships. Chapters 4 through 8 analyze the effects of reform in the five states. In each case we describe the state's prereform and postreform school finance systems; discuss prereform-to-postreform changes in the distribution of fiscal outcomes and fiscal capacities and efforts and in the relative positions of various types of school districts; and end with comments on how various aspects of the state's plan seem to have affected reform outcomes. Finally, Chapter 9 contrasts the results of reform across the five states, draws some general conclusions on what these reform plans have and have not accomplished, and speculates on why these plans led to the observed results. Carroll (1979) provides additional statistical information on the prereform and postreform distributions and relationships in each state.

2 PRINCIPAL FINDINGS

The study's principal findings for each state are briefly summarized below. More comprehensive summaries for the individual states are presented at the ends of Chapters 4 through 8. Interstate comparisons are drawn in Chapter 9, which also includes a more extensive discussion of our general conclusions and some speculations on why these reforms yielded the outcomes they did.

REFORM PLANS IN THE SAMPLE STATES

The reform plans in California, Florida, Kansas, Michigan, and New Mexico reflect diverse views of what reform entails.

California combined a high-level foundation plan [1] with differential growth limits on expenditures. The foundation program very substantially increased state aid to low-wealth districts, while the expenditure growth limits permitted greater expenditure increases to lower spending districts. Different foundation levels, computational tax rates, and growth allowances are provided for elementary, secondary, and unified districts.

---

[1] The typical foundation plan guarantees that each district will end up with a minimum amount of funding per pupil (the foundation level) at a stipulated property tax rate. A district's state aid is the difference between the foundation level and the amount per pupil that the district could raise locally at the specified rate. See Chapter 3 for details and illustrations.

Districts may seek voter approval for tax overrides. If successful, their expenditures may exceed their growth limit by the amount of local revenues generated by the additional tax levy.

Florida also retained the foundation program approach. The reform plan incorporates a very extensive system of adjustments for the distribution of a district's pupils among twenty-six different categories, and an adjustment for the cost of living in the county served by a district. Local districts are limited to a narrow range of tax rates.

Kansas adopted a guaranteed tax base (GTB) plan constrained by strict limits on expenditure growth and tied, in a complex fashion, to "norm" budgets.[2] The growth limits allow districts spending below the norm to increase their budgets more rapidly than can districts spending above the norm. The state's districts are divided into three enrollment categories; different norm budgets are specified for each category.

Michigan introduced an unrestricted GTB plan with an upper bound on the number of mills for which state aid is paid. Districts may levy higher rates.

New Mexico has assumed full responsibility for school finance, while retaining the local district as the operating unit. The New Mexico plan allows no local discretion on district revenues or tax rates. A pupil-weighting system with adjustments for teacher cost differentials is used to determine each district's budget, and the schools are financed out of state funds plus a state-mandated local levy.

These five plans do not represent alternative approaches to a common objective of equity, unless "equity" is defined so vaguely as to be an operationally meaningless term. Michigan's plan, for example, is clearly oriented toward providing more equal fiscal opportunities, defined as per pupil revenues per mill levied, and does nothing to impose a more equal distribution of fiscal outcomes on the state's school districts (though the choices they make may, of course, result in a distribution of fiscal outcomes more equal than the one prevailing before reform). New Mexico's plan seems designed to equalize fiscal outcomes, defined in terms of tax rates and the degree to which a district's real re-

---

[2]The terms "guaranteed tax base" and "variable matching" are generally used to refer to a formula that ensures to each district a minimum revenue per pupil for each percentage point of tax effort. "District power equalizing" (DPE) generally refers to a plan that also allows each district no more than the guaranteed amount of revenue per unit of tax effort. That is, a DPE plan is a GTB plan with full recapture of "excess" local revenue by the state. For further details, see Barro (1974).

sources (i.e., adjusted for cost differences) are matched to its students' needs.

California, Florida, and Kansas opted for what can be construed as compromise plans: Each allows a local district limited discretion in selecting its budget and tax rate. The Kansas plan attempts to reduce inequality in the distribution of per-pupil budgets by more severely limiting revenue growth in higher spending districts. At the same time, it fiscally neutralizes whatever spending differences remain. The division of districts into three categories can be viewed as a cost adjustment to compensate for economies of scale.

California and Florida also have imposed limits on revenue growth rates and tax rates, respectively, which, coupled with their foundation programs' floors on spending, seem designed to reduce inequities in fiscal outcomes. Both states appear to define fiscal outcomes in terms of tax rates and pupil needs. (California's tripartite system can be interpreted as a response to the differential needs of elementary and high school students.) And Florida's adjustment for intercounty differences in the cost of living can be interpreted as an adjustment for resource cost differences. Although neither state attempts to fiscally neutralize the expenditure differentials permitted within its plan, the floor imposed by the foundation program, coupled with the revenue or tax limit, constrains the degree to which high-wealth districts are able to take advantage of their fiscal capacities. In this sense, California and Florida limit wealth bias in their school financing systems.

Depending on one's point of view, revenue or tax rate limits may be interpreted as devices for bringing about gradual equalization, for delaying equalization, for limiting disparities in a system that permits local discretion, for controlling the cost of state aid, or for forcing local districts to translate a part of their state aid into local property tax relief.

THE EFFECTS OF REFORM IN CALIFORNIA

California's reform plan has had moderate success in reducing disparities in the distribution of revenues per pupil.[3] Among unified dis-

---

[3]Revenues equal the sum of local revenues, state noncategorical aid, and federal impact aid. This measure, in our view, best reflects the concepts expressed in the reform debate. Readers with different views or who are interested in the effects of categorical programs will find parallel analyses for alternative revenue measures that exclude impact aid or include state or federal categorical aid in the detailed analyses of the individual states. See Chapters 4 through 8.

tricts, disparities have been reduced by 32 to 36 percent. Elementary school districts also experienced declines in revenue disparities, on the order of 20 percent. Reform has not greatly reduced disparities among students in high school districts, and has had little effect on disparities in the distribution of instructional expenditures per pupil among districts of any type. Finally, the postreform years have seen substantially reduced disparities in tax rates among districts of all three types.

Wealth neutrality has been improved by reform, but revenues remain highly dependent on property tax bases in all three types of districts. Income neutrality has been improved even more, but income also continues to be closely associated with school districts' revenues. There have been slight increases in the degree to which the revenues of high school and unified districts are solely determined by their tax rates, and there has been a substantial increase in the association between elementary school districts' tax rates and their revenues. All in all, after reform, school districts of all types found their revenues somewhat more dependent on their fiscal efforts and less dependent on the size of their tax base and the income of their community.

Reform has not profoundly affected the distribution of revenues or instructional expenditures between large and small, more urban and less urban, more white and less white, or more poverty-prone and less poverty-prone districts. The distribution of tax rates, however, changed considerably. Larger elementary and high school districts decreased tax rates relative to their smaller counterparts, but the larger unified districts increased theirs relative to smaller unified districts. The same pattern by district type holds for the less urban and the more urban districts. Tax rates in all types of districts rose higher in less white communities than they did in more white communities. In all three types of districts, tax rates declined in districts serving less poverty-prone populations relative to districts serving more poverty-prone populations.

THE EFFECTS OF REFORM IN FLORIDA

Florida's reform widened disparities in both revenues per pupil and instructional expenditures per pupil.

Reform led to a substantially less fiscally neutral finance system, marked by a considerably closer association between per-pupil revenues and wealth, and between instructional expenditures per pupil and wealth. Before reform, districts' per-pupil revenues and instructional expenditures were independent of the incomes of the communities they served. Since reform, a highly significant relationship has prevailed between each revenue and expenditure variable and household income per pupil. Finally, reform saw substantial declines in the relationship between revenues and instructional expenditures, on the one hand, and tax rates, on the other. School districts' revenues and instructional expenditures are less closely related to their tax efforts after reform than they were before.

Florida's reform has benefited the larger and the more urban districts more than it has the smaller and the less urban districts, and has very substantially benefited districts serving communities in which a relatively small proportion of the population is poverty-prone.

THE EFFECTS OF REFORM IN KANSAS

Prior to reform, state general aid to the schools in Kansas was delivered through a foundation plan to which a supplementary aid program had been appended. A district's state aid was based on its enrollment, the characteristics of its certified employees, and a county-wide economic index prorated to the district according to its share of the certified employees in the county. The 1973 reform introduced a GTB program. School districts were limited in their annual budget increases to the lower of 15 percent of the previous year's budget or 5 percent of the median budget per pupil for Kansas districts in the same enrollment category.

Revenues per pupil were somewhat more equally distributed in Kansas after reform than they were before, particularly in the large districts. Disparities in the distribution of revenues declined 5 to 10 percent among the small and medium-sized districts and 15 to 20 percent among the large districts. Reform left the distribution of instructional expenditures per pupil virtually unchanged among small and medium districts, but for the large districts, disparities declined by about 18 percent. The distributions of adjusted tax rates, however, became much more equal for all types of districts; disparities fell by roughly one-third.

Kansas reform has had little effect on fiscal neutrality. It did little to change associations between per pupil revenues or instructional expenditures and the property tax base. Revenues and instructional expenditures were somewhat more closely related to household income per pupil after reform than they had been before. The tax rate was unrelated to revenues or expenditures in either year among the small districts; it was slightly related to them both before and after reform for medium-sized districts, and in the postreform years for the large districts.

Among small districts, reform's big winners were the urban districts, the less white districts, and those where the incidence of poverty was lower. The distributions of revenues and instructional expenditures among different kinds of medium and large districts were not much affected by reform.

THE EFFECTS OF REFORM IN MICHIGAN

Revenue disparities remained about the same in Michigan following reform, but disparities in tax rates declined substantially.

For fiscal neutrality, the results are mixed. The postreform years saw much more income neutrality and substantial increases in the degree to which revenues depended on the tax rate. But wealth neutrality appears greater only in comparison with one prereform year, 1972; compared with another, 1971, the postreform years show little improvement.

Finally, reform has had little effect on the distributions of revenues among various kinds of districts or on the distributions of tax rates between large and small, urban and nonurban, and disproportionately white and nonwhite districts. Districts in which the incidence of poverty was relatively low levied considerably lower taxes before reform; after reform, they still levied lower taxes but their relative advantage has been much reduced.

What did not happen in Michigan as a result of reform is as interesting as what did. Michigan's reform plan placed no restrictions on a district's choice of budget level (and tax rate). Districts with a stronger "taste" for education than for other public and private goods and services could levy high local taxes and generate high revenues. Districts that preferred to keep taxes (and school budgets) lower were free to do so. This newfound freedom produced no dramatic contrasts in district behavior, however. If anything, revenues are somewhat more equally distributed after reform than they were before, and the disparities in local tax rates have substantially lessened.

THE EFFECTS OF REFORM IN NEW MEXICO

Reform in New Mexico has reduced disparities in revenues per pupil but not in instructional expenditures per pupil. The improvement in the revenue distribution largely reflects one key provision of the reform plan: Public Law (PL) 874 revenues are counted against a district's state aid. The remaining provisions of the plan, including the state's complete assumption of school finance responsibilities, account for only a small decline in revenue disparities. It appears that the primary effect of the reform on distributional equality has been to "equalize" PL 874 revenues.

Fiscal neutrality has generally improved, but wealth remains a significant predictor of revenues and of instructional expenditures. Reform also improved income neutrality. The state-mandated local property tax levy fully eliminates any relationship between local tax effort and school districts' revenues or instructional expenditures.

The larger, the more urban, and the more white districts have gained on their smaller, less urban, and less white counterparts. But the gains have been small, and the larger and more urban districts still have lower average revenues and instructional expenditures. After reform, average revenues and expenditures in the districts serving less white populations were generally lower than in the districts serving more white populations. The reverse had been true before reform. None of these shifts have been large, however.

CONCLUSIONS

Our results suggest that reform efforts in these five states have brought about only slightly more equal distributions of per-pupil revenues; nor have they reduced disparities in instructional expenditures per pupil by much, if at all. However, reform has led to more equal distributions of tax rates.

Reform has improved wealth neutrality; in general, both revenues and instructional expenditures per pupil are less closely related to property tax bases after reform than they were before. While income neutrality improved in some cases, the distributions of revenues and of instructional expenditures per pupil are in other cases more income-biased after reform than they were before. In many cases, reform tightened the relationship between local districts' tax efforts and their revenues and instructional expenditures per pupil; however, in other cases, that relationship has worsened with reform.

What kinds of districts and students gained from reform? Who lost? Our results suggest that, with rare exceptions, reform has not affected the distributions of per-pupil revenues, instructional expenditures, or tax rates among different kinds of districts. The one set of results that reveals substantial effects from reform suggests that tax rates have generally fallen in districts where the incidence of poverty is low relative to those where it is high. In numerous instances, reform brought about a more equal distribution of tax rates.

All in all, reforms in these five states have not dramatically reduced the problems that originally gave rise to pressures for school finance reform. There has been considerable progress, but on the whole, each state's postreform distributions of revenues and instructional expenditures are remarkably similar to what they were before. From the perspective of tax equity, however, these reforms appear to have been quite successful. In every case except Florida, disparities in tax rates have narrowed dramatically. Reform seems to have been an effective device for equalizing the burdens of supporting education.

3 VARIABLES AND MEASURES

"Diverse" is the word for all aspects of the debate over school finance reform. Proponents and opponents of reform have raised an array of issues; previous studies of the effects of reform in one state or another have examined diverse kinds of outcomes; and the reform plans thus far implemented seem oriented toward disparate goals. People differ widely over the particular outcomes or opportunities whose distributions should be the central concern, and equally widely over what constitutes "success" in this context.

This chapter details the particular reform outcomes we have selected for study. We review some of the issues that have figured in the reform debate. We then define the variables we used as indicators of reform outcomes. Finally, we describe the statistical measures we used to summarize distributions of fiscal outcomes and opportunities.

BACKGROUND

The distributional shortcomings of the prereform school finance plans have been exhaustively documented both in the research literature and in the massive evidence compiled for the school finance cases.[1]

[1]Wise (1968) and Coons, Clune, and Sugarman (1970) provide seminal statements of the problem. Brown et al.(1977) summarize the disparities in expenditures and the relations between disparities and local wealth in each of the fifty states.

The main source of financial inequality under the systems that prevailed in nearly all states before 1970, and that still prevail in many states, is the interaction between local property taxation and methods of distributing state aid.

Prior to 1970, the most common state school finance plan was based on the concept of the foundation program.[2] The typical foundation system guarantees that each district will end up with at least a minimum amount of funding per pupil (the foundation level) at a stipulated property tax rate. A district's state aid is the difference (if greater than zero) between the foundation level and the amount per pupil that the district could raise locally at the specified rate. Most states using a foundation plan require that a district's property tax rate be at least as large as the stipulated rate if it is to receive any aid.

Foundation plans are equalizing to the extent that they give all districts equal access to the foundation level. In nearly all prereform instances, however, the foundation level had been set far below the statewide average level of spending per pupil, and districts were left to make up the difference by drawing on their own highly unequal property tax bases. And foundation plans do nothing to equalize the differences between "in-plan" districts and districts so wealthy that their local levy at the stipulated rate exceeds the foundation level.

To illustrate, consider two districts whose assessed values per pupil are $20,000 and $10,000. Suppose the foundation level is set at $500 per pupil at a tax rate of 2 percent (20 mills). The wealthier district would receive a grant of $100 per pupil ($500 minus 0.02 times $20,000) and the poorer a grant of $300 ($500 minus 0.02 times $10,000). Each district would thus be able to provide a $500 per pupil educational program at a tax rate of 2 percent. But the formula does nothing to compensate for differences in local ability to augment the foundation program. If the same two districts taxed themselves at a rate of 4 percent, the wealthier would be able to spend $900 per pupil ($800 raised locally plus $100 in state aid) while the poorer could spend only $700 ($400 in local revenues plus $300 in state aid). Or, to achieve a spending level of, say, $1,000 per pupil, the wealthier district would need a tax rate of only 4.5 percent; the poorer district would have to impose a 7 percent rate to do as well. A third district, whose assessed property value per student was $50,000, would receive no aid; but it

[2]For a more detailed explanation of the foundation program, see Barro (1974). According to the National Educational Finance Project (1971), thirty-four states operated foundation-type systems in 1968–69.

could raise $2,000 per pupil at a 4 percent levy and would need to levy only 2 percent to raise $1,000 per pupil.

Several states operated flat-grant distribution schemes.[3] These plans equalize only to the extent that districts' revenues are not entirely dependent on local resources.

A few states, prior to 1970, had adopted plans with features similar to those now advocated by reformers, including matching grant plans of the "percentage-equalizing" type. However, the operation of these formulas was typically so hemmed in by constraints (aid floors and ceilings, limits on matching rates, etc.) that the results were scarcely distinguishable from those under the more conventional foundation and flat-grant systems.[4]

Three features of the foundation plans, working in combination, produced both unequal financial opportunities and unequal outcomes: First, local school districts were left to depend on their own property taxes for the portion of revenue not provided by the state. Second, in many states the amount of locally taxable property per pupil varies drastically among districts. Third, state aid funds have not been distributed in a way that compensates for interdistrict tax base disparities, even under systems supposedly designed to equalize resources among districts. The school finance reforms of the 1970s were designed to remedy these shortcomings.

REFORM THEMES

We have discussed the two main themes that pervade the debate over school finance systems: equality of fiscal outcomes and fiscal neutrality, or the equality of fiscal opportunities. Each theme subsumes a number of approaches to reform, depending on how one defines fiscal outcomes or opportunities. In either case, for example, there is the question of whether outcomes or opportunities should be measured in terms of dollars per pupil, school resources per pupil, or the extent to which each pupil's needs are met. Some reform plans simply focus on district funding; others focus on funding levels adjusted for presumed

[3]According to the National Educational Finance Project (1971), seven states distributed flat amounts of aid per pupil in 1968–69.

[4]For example, see the descriptions of the New York, Massachusetts, and Rhode Island plans in U.S. Office of Education (1972).

interdistrict differences in the costs of school resources or in the proportion of pupils who are "expensive to educate" or who have special needs. And there is the question of which revenues or expenditures should be included in the measurement of outcomes or opportunities: all categories of per-pupil funding regardless of source or purpose; funds received from some sources (e.g., local revenues and state general aid) but not from others (e.g., state and federal categorical grants); funds employed for certain purposes (e.g., current operations) but not for others (e.g., capital outlays); and so forth.

Fiscal limits or constraints have also played an important role in the reform debate. Many states have imposed limits on school districts' revenues or tax levies as a part of their reform plan. In some cases, the school finance reform plan was enacted as a part of a larger bill addressing tax issues. California's 1973 reform, for example, was included in Senate Bill 90, which imposed revenue limits on all local governments: cities, counties, and special districts, as well as school districts.

FISCAL OUTCOMES

Educational outcomes (e.g., pupils' achievement) and educational quality have also figured in the reform debate. As a practical matter, however, we lack methods for accurately measuring educational outcomes or quality. Furthermore, reform proponents have frequently argued that the effects of reform on educational quality, however measured, are irrelevant. Equality of educational opportunity, in this view, requires only that students have equal access to educational resources, regardless of how those resources contribute to achievement.

The fiscal outcomes discussed in the context of reform differ from one another in two respects: adjustments for the financial circumstances of school districts (or taxpayers), and the scope of the outcomes.

Adjustments for Districts' (Taxpayers') Financial Circumstances

The distribution of expenditures (or revenues) per pupil is a widely shared reform concern. It rests on the straightforward philosophical base of treating all students alike, regardless of their, or their districts', characteristics, and poses minimal measurement problems. State aid formulas oriented toward this concern are easily devised, and interested parties—including the courts—can readily verify the degree of equalization that has been achieved.

Critics, however, argue that dollars have little to do with educational equity. The school resources—teachers, books, materials, facilities, and so forth—available to students are what matter. Accordingly, equality needs to be measured by the quantity and quality of resources that students receive. If there are interdistrict differences in resource costs, the distribution of funding per pupil does not reflect the distribution of resources per pupil. Thus, concern should focus on funding per pupil adjusted for resource cost differentials.

The practical difficulties of measuring resource costs are severe. We lack means for assessing the quality of most school resources, particularly teachers, who account for the large majority of school expenditures. For example, the average teacher's salary in a district reflects the experience and education distribution of the teacher force. If a teacher's experience and education do not enhance the quality of the educational process, it is appropriate to adjust for the cost of maintaining a more experienced or educated, but not higher quality, teacher force. But suppose experience and education improve a teacher's quality. Then, differences in teachers' salaries that result from differences in their experience and education reflect differences in teacher quality and do not imply resource cost differences. In this case, cost adjustment is not appropriate. Similarly, the level of a district's teacher salary schedule—the salary paid to teachers with given amounts of experience and education—includes both the cost of obtaining a teacher with given characteristics and any premium the district may be willing to pay to attract and retain particularly able people. Consequently, the funding of districts that pay higher teacher salaries should be cost-adjusted if we can establish that they are not thereby attracting higher quality teachers.

There has been considerable debate over whether reform should focus on the provision of inputs (either dollars or resources) or on the extent to which pupils' needs are met. The latter view is based on the argument that the purpose of schooling is to further students' education and that some students (e.g., the disadvantaged, handicapped, learning disabled) require more resources if they are to progress as rapidly as their peers. In other words, if equity demands that equals receive equal treatment, then unequals (in the sense of educational needs) must receive unequal (compensatory) treatment. The growth of federal and state compensatory education programs testifies to the appeal of this principle. But the practical problems of measuring students' needs and translating the measurements into an aid allocation formula are even more severe than those encountered in constructing educational cost indexes.

It is difficult to conceive of an operational definition of educational need that is not linked to some measurable index of performance or outcome; but the education community has yet to agree on the outcomes or competencies that the schools should impart to students, or even to define many dimensions of performance. Moreover, we lack accurate means for measuring most of those performance criteria whose importance is a matter of agreement. For example, few would deny that cognitive achievement is important, and procedures for testing it are far more advanced than the methods used to test for other educational outcomes. Nonetheless, the accuracy of cognitive achievement tests is continually questioned; and even if it were not, our knowledge of the relationships between resources and outcomes is so fragmentary and conflicting that statements regarding the amounts of resources needed by some kinds of students (to keep pace with their peers or to achieve some performance objective) are virtually meaningless.[5]

The pupil-weighting systems thus far proposed or implemented are essentially equivalent to categorical aid programs appended to a system that equalizes general funds or resources per pupil. Students are categorized according to perceptions of their needs, each category is assigned a weight, and funding (or resources) per weighted student is equalized. An identical result could be obtained by equalizing funding (or resources) per unweighted student and installing a set of categorical programs that funded category i students at a rate equal to the product of the category i weight minus one and the equalized general funding per pupil.[6] Thus, all the problems of determining an appro-

---

[5]See Averch et al. (1974) for a discussion of this point.

[6]Florida (in 1975–76), for example, assigned a weight of 1.0 to fourth through ninth graders, 1.1 to tenth, eleventh, and twelfth graders, 2.3 to the educable mentally retarded, and so forth, for twenty-six different student categories. Each district is equalized at $745 (times a cost adjustment factor) per weighted pupil. An identical result would be obtained from a system that equalized the cost-adjusted sum of $745 per unweighted pupil, and provided $74.50 in categorical funds (0.1 x $745) for each tenth through twelfth grader, $968.50 in categorical funds (1.3 × $745) for each educable mentally retarded student, and so forth for all twenty-six student categories.

priate compensatory education system are encountered in developing a pupil-weighting, or student-need-adjusted, finance plan.

As a practical matter, pupil-weighting systems may have little effect on the distribution of resources among a state's school districts. If every district's pupils are distributed among the weighting categories in roughly the same proportion, the weighting process will have a negligible effect on the distribution of per-pupil revenues among the districts. Formally, if a state's system assigns a weight of α_i to category i pupils, the jth district's entitlement (in a plan like New Mexico's) or foundation (in a plan like Florida's) will be $\gamma N_j \sum_{i=1}^{n} \alpha_i p_{ij}$, where γ is the entitlement or foundation per weighted pupil, p_{ij} is the proportion of the jth district's pupils who are in category i, and N_j is the total number of pupils in the jth district. If the p_{ij}'s are constant across districts, the entitlement for the jth district can be written $\alpha N_j K$, where $K = \sum_{i=1}^{n} \alpha_i p_{ij}$ is a constant. In other words, a support level of γK per (unweighted) pupil would have yielded precisely the same outcome.

Florida's system is a good example of this point. The simple correlation between its districts' weighted and unweighted pupils was 0.9997 in 1975. There is not one district in the state in which the aggregate pupil weight is significantly different from (approximately) 1.26 times the number of pupils. If the state had entirely dispensed with its pupil-weighting system and simply set each district's foundation 1.26 times $745 per (unweighted) pupil, it would have obtained almost exactly the same distribution of fiscal outcomes.

The Scope of Concern

Fiscal outcomes, however defined, may encompass all categories of per-pupil funding or apply only to support from certain sources or for certain functions. The objective could be as broad as minimizing variation in districts' total expenditures per pupil or as narrow as reducing disparities in the per-pupil amount spent for teachers. Thus far, attention has centered on current support per pupil: Most descriptions of prereform systems emphasize interdistrict variations in current support per pupil; most of the reform plans implemented to date make no attempt to equalize debt service or capital outlays; and studies of their effects focus on improvements in the distribution of per-pupil current revenues or expenditures.

The most troublesome issues raised by the question, "To what categories of funding or expenditures should equalization apply?" concern capital expenditures, revenues derived from state and federal categorical aid programs, and the distinction between revenues and expenditures.

In most states, debt service and capital outlays are supported by local property taxes and by state aid programs that are only mildly equalizing at best. Access to capital funds is as inequitably distributed as access to funds for the support of current operations. And there is no reason why the former should be of less concern than the latter. However, the conceptual and practical problems of addressing reform issues in the capital account have thus far proved insurmountable.

Conceptually, a district's physical facilities and equipment are a stock built up through the accumulation of past net investment flows. Past investment decisions, in turn, reflect the district's ability to obtain investments funds and its decisions regarding tradeoffs between capital and other school inputs. Because capital overlays and debt service are largely financed through property taxes, districts with large per-pupil tax bases could raise more funds at a given tax rate than could their less wealthy counterparts and, other things equal, would have accumulated a relatively larger capital stock over past years. But other things may not have been equal. One district may have chosen to make do with older facilities and equipment in order to "afford" a larger teaching force; another may have contented itself with fewer teachers per pupil, transferring funds from current account to capital account and modernizing old facilities or building new ones. At any time, then, districts' capital stocks per pupil are likely to be unequal. Disparities between districts are partially due to past inequities in access to capital funds and partially due to differences in their past evaluations of the relative importance of facilities and other school inputs.

Equalization or fiscal neutralization of districts' capital outlays and debt service would affect only their relative access to funds for additions to, and replacements of, their current capital stocks. With the passage of time, of course, districts' current capital stocks will "run down" and eventually be entirely replaced by new investment. But equalization of access to investment funds would do nothing to equalize existing disparities in capital stocks. In fact, if the schools' capital stock is long-lived—and past experience suggests that school facilities are often used for many decades—equalization of investment may freeze existing disparities by precluding "catching up" by capital-poor districts. Reform on capital account therefore must address both disparities in access to future capital funds and disparities in existing capital stocks, to the extent that they reflect past inequities in access to capital funds.

At present, because we do not have methods for assessing the quality of a district's capital stock, we cannot measure interdistrict disparities in capital stocks. Even if we could, we would still need some method for determining the extent to which those disparities stem from past inequities in access to capital funds. (It would be inequitable to equalize capital stock disparities if they result from past district choices among school inputs.) But we have no such method. In sum, we lack the means for addressing reform issues with respect to capital outlay and debt service funds.

All federal aid to elementary and secondary education and approximately 15 percent of state support for the schools are distributed through categorical aid programs. In all, these programs account for nearly 15 percent of public education's total revenues. Most school districts derive some support from these programs, and they are a major source of many districts' revenues.

Somewhat surprisingly, in view of their importance, the equalization debate has paid little attention to these programs. Most of the studies that concentrate on the distribution of current revenues exclude funds from federal aid programs. But some include receipts from state categorical programs, while others exclude them. The studies that concentrate on the distribution of current expenditures implicitly include categorical aid, willy-nilly, to the extent that categorical programs contribute to the support of current operations. Few studies of either type offer any explanation for their treatment of categorical revenues.

State legislators' views appear to be equally diverse. Most of the reform plans entirely neglect federal aid—presumably because equalization does not extend to federal revenues. Kansas and New Mexico, however, adjust a district's general aid for receipt of impact aid, that is, Public Law (PL) 874, funds. Similarly, as noted above, pupil-weighting systems are equivalent to appending a package of categorical programs to an equalized general aid program. Thus, states opting for pupil-weighting systems formally extend the concept of equalization to all state aid, including both general and categorical aid, while those who maintain a separate system of categorical programs presumably exclude them in considering the equalization issue. In any event, there is no general agreement as to how categorical programs should be treated in assessing interdistrict funding disparities.

Should reform focus on the distribution of revenues or on the distribution of expenditures? The question is moot if equalization extends to all categories of funding: Total revenues equal total expenditures plus increases (minus decreases) in balances, and the latter are negligible relative to total revenues or expenditures. At lower levels of aggregations, revenues are generally categorized by source while expenditures are categorized by use. There are no expenditure categories corresponding to, say, local revenues or state noncategorical aid, and no revenue categories corresponding to, say, instructional expenditures or spending for teachers. Consequently, the decision to focus on some measure of support that is less inclusive than current revenues or expenditures precludes a choice between a revenue-oriented measure and an expenditure-oriented measure. But there is an important difference between current revenues and current expenditures. Because current support per pupil is the most common focus of equalization efforts and analyses, the choice between a revenue-oriented measure and an expenditure-oriented measure is significant.

All states preclude transfers of funds from capital account to current account, but most permit transfers from current account to capital expenditures, and the difference can be significant. If the rate at which districts transfer funds from current to capital account is related to their per-pupil revenues, the distribution of revenue per pupil may noticeably differ from the distribution of per-pupil expenditures.

Suppose, for example, that districts with high revenues per pupil devote a disproportionate share of their funds to the improvement of plant and equipment, while districts with low revenues per pupil find that current operating expenditures consume a large share of their funds. This would be the case if districts generally viewed improved plant and equipment as luxuries to be indulged in only after current operations are supported at an "adequate" level. Then, the distribution of current expenditures would be much more equal than the distribution of current revenues. More generally, a state that appears to be fairly equalized, using distribution of current expenditures as the criterion, can appear to be far less equalized if distribution of current revenues is the criterion.

Adjustments to and Scope of Tax Burdens

For concreteness, the above discussion focused on fiscal outcomes pertaining to the distribution of resources among school districts. A parallel set of arguments applies to the distribution of tax burdens among taxpayers.

The most straightforward measure of tax burdens is the local property tax levied for education. But, some argue, the important issue is the share of individual income that goes for school taxes. Adjustments for differences in incomes are needed, in this view, to accurately portray the distribution of tax burdens.

Although that argument has merit, the practical problems of adjusting for income differences are insurmountable. In theory, a part of the property tax levied on commercial and industrial properties is borne by the owners and the remainder is passed on to renters and consumers, but research has yet to measure the comparative burdens on the two groups. Consequently, whose incomes should be related to what degrees of property tax burdens remains an unanswered question.

Many states permit school districts to levy several different taxes in support of current operations, capital outlay and debt services, and various special funds. Is the sum of all local levies the central interest, or only the taxes levied for certain purposes? The issue exactly parallels the problem of including or excluding revenues (or expenditures) for certain purposes.

FISCAL NEUTRALITY

The concept of fiscal neutrality focuses on districts' access to revenues. A school finance system is said to be fiscally neutral if each district's funding per pupil (possibly adjusted for cost and need differentials) depends solely on its fiscal efforts and is independent of its wealth or ability to pay. Note that neutrality does not require equality in funding (or adjusted funding) per pupil. Rather, it requires that any district be able to obtain the same (adjusted) funding per pupil as any other district provided only that it put forth the same effort.

It is generally agreed that equity requires fiscal neutrality. A system that results in equal (adjusted) funding per pupil but places unequal fiscal burdens on local districts is clearly inequitable. And to many reform advocates, fiscal neutrality is sufficient for equity. That is, equity is satisfied if all districts have an equal opportunity to obtain funds regardless of the extent to which they take advantage of their opportunities. District power-equalizing (DPE) plans, for example, derive from this concept of equity. And, from this point of view, fiscal neutrality itself becomes the equalization target.

Practical application of fiscal neutrality raises the question of how to define "ability of pay" or "fiscal effort" or "wealth." In its early days, the reform movement focused on the relationship between a district's funding and its tax base. The local school property tax rate came to be equated with effort, and "wealth" was the property tax base per pupil. Operationally, fiscal neutrality came to mean that pupil support could (in fact, should) vary with the property tax rate, but not with the property tax base. As the finance debate matured, however, the original definitions of fiscal effort and wealth have been questioned and new definitions proposed. A natural extension is to define both wealth and effort more comprehensively. Kansas, for example, includes income in the definition of wealth, and defines effort in terms of local school revenues relative to income plus property tax base.

An important conceptual distinction needs to be made between ex ante and ex post definitions of fiscal neutrality. Ex ante neutrality exists where a given level of fiscal effort provides the same per-pupil revenue to each district regardless of local wealth, as under a pure DPE formula. Ex post neutrality exists where actual per-pupil spending and wealth are uncorrelated.

The two concepts of fiscal neutrality are not equivalent, and systems that satisfy one may fail to satisfy the other. Suppose, for example, that high-wealth communities are more willing to tax themselves for the schools even when they are not permitted to take advantage of their greater ability to raise revenues at a given tax rate (perhaps because people who choose to live in such communities prize education above private and other public goods and services, or because they enjoyed high levels of per-pupil school support prior to reform and are unwilling or unable to revise school budgets downward). In an ex ante fiscally neutral system (e.g., a pure DPE system), such communities would impose greater tax burdens on themselves, and thereby obtain greater per-pupil funding for their schools. The resulting correlation between wealth and per-pupil support would violate ex post fiscal neutrality even though it emerged from an ex ante fiscally neutral system. Conversely, suppose that people, regardless of where they lived, generally agreed on the "right" amount of per-pupil support for the schools and were willing to exert whatever efforts were needed to provide that amount of support, but unwilling to exert themselves much beyond that point. In a flat-grant system, or a foundation system that set the foundation well below the support level, high-wealth communities would levy low tax rates while lower wealth communities levied higher tax rates. All communities would thereby end up with about the same level of per-pupil funding and the correlation between funding and wealth might be negligible. Thus, ex post fiscal neutrality would be satisfied even though the system clearly violated ex ante fiscal neutrality.

VARIABLES OF INTEREST

To accommodate the disparate views of the proper objective of reform, we examine the effects of each state's reform on several measures of current revenues per pupil, on instructional expenditures per pupil, and on local property taxes levied for education.

Current Revenue Per Pupil

We examine only current per-pupil revenues and entirely disregard capital outlays and debt service. Because variations in access to revenues, however measured, are the central issue, we believe that variations in current revenues are more meaningful than variations in current expenditures. This choice also reflects the lack of adequate procedures, and data, for addressing capital disparities.

States often require that districts segregate earmarked revenues in separate accounts. These typically include aid from federal and state categorical programs and local revenues derived from special property taxes. Although these funds may be used only for the specified purpose, they nonetheless contribute to the support of current operations. Accordingly, we aggregate over all accounts (other than capital outlay and debt service) in computing current revenues per pupil.

We examine five alternative measures of current revenues, exclusive and inclusive of receipts from various categorical programs. Readers with different views of what should be equalized may find one of these measures compatible with their values. This also allows us to assess the consequences of evaluating equalization outcomes from more than one perspective. Finally, the use of alternative measures will permit comparison of our results with those obtained in other studies. The measures are:

General revenue per pupil. This measure comprises the sum of local revenue, intermediate revenue (e.g., from a county), and state non-categorical revenue. We net out all state program support, even if included in the state's basic aid formula, and include all noncategorical aid, even if distributed independently of basic aid. This variable indicates the amount of nonfederal funds available to the district that it can spend entirely at its own discretion.

General plus PL 874 revenue per pupil. The federal impact aid program (PL 874) distributes funds to districts that are heavily affected by the presence of federal installations and employees within their boundaries. The ostensible purpose is to compensate districts for the burden of educating the children of families who work, and often live, on tax-exempt property. Although it is a categorical aid program, the funds it provides can be viewed as substituting for "lost" local revenues. Two of the states we study, Kansas and New Mexico, explicitly adopt this view, adjusting state general aid for a district's PL 874 receipts. This variable includes local, intermediate, state noncategorical, and federal PL 874 revenue. It indicates the total amount of discretionary funds per pupil that is available to each district.

Local plus state revenue per pupil. Our third current revenue variable is the sum of all nonfederal revenue per pupil. It includes all revenue from local, intermediate, and state sources, and excludes all revenue from federal sources, including federal aid channeled through states (e.g., aid provided through the Elementary and Secondary Education Act, PL 89–10)

Local plus state plus PL 874 revenue per pupil. Aside from impact aid, all major (and most minor) federal aid programs regulate districts' uses of federal funds. This variable, the sum of all nonfederal revenues plus impact aid per pupil, corresponds to the amount of per-pupil funds available to a district that are not constrained by federal regulation.[7]

Total revenue per pupil. The fifth revenue variable is total current revenue per pupil from all sources—local, intermediate, state, and federal.

Instructional Expenditures Per Pupil

Schools devote more than 40 percent of their total revenue to support activities other than instruction, including administration, plant opera-

---

[7]Federal programs do constrain districts' uses of nonfederal funds to the extent that supplementation, maintenance of effort, and similar regulations limit a district's ability to shift local revenues away from the activities or pupils to which federal aid is targeted.

tion and maintenance, capital outlay, debt service, and other activities. These activities are necessary, but the schools' primary purpose is education, and the central purpose of reform efforts is to rectify disparities in the quality of education offered to students living in different districts. From this perspective, the effects of reform on disparities in instructional expenditures are a major concern. Accordingly, the sixth variable we examine is instructional expenditures per pupil—the sum of direct expenditures for instruction, and expenditures for instructional support services, including pupil personnel, instructional media, instructional and curriculum development, and instructional staff development and training.

Adjusted Tax Rates

Discussions of school finance inequalities generally express the issue in the context of educational equity, but the issue can equally well be posed in terms of tax equity. That is, taxpayers are treated inequitably when the tax burdens they must shoulder to provide a given level of education to their communities' children depend on where they live. Advocates of fiscal neutrality as the equalization objective essentially adopt this position in that they consider inequalities in revenues perfectly acceptable as long as they result from inequalities in the tax burdens that communities choose to bear.

We examine the effects of each state's reform on the distribution of adjusted local property tax rates. The variable is the sum of all local and intermediate property tax rates whose levies support the schools' current operations times the ratio of assessed value to market value. It includes the general- (or operational-) fund tax rate and any special-fund, current-account tax rates (e.g., for a Social Security fund) and excludes capital outlay and debt service tax rates. To facilitate interstate comparisons, we convert nominal tax rates—which are levied on assessed values—to the rate effectively levied on market value. District-specific ratios of assessed market values are used where available; otherwise, we use statewide ratios. Tax rates are expressed in mills, that is, tenths of a percent.

WEIGHTS

We were, and are, inclined to the view that the student is the appropriate unit of analysis. However, we recognized that interdistrict disparities are also of interest and computed each of our measures twice, first ascertaining the values unweighted, and then weighting the value of a variable in each district by its size. We concentrate on the pupil-weighted results in our analysis. Both sets of results are presented in Carroll (1979); the reader interested in the effects of reform on districts (as opposed to students) will find the relevant measures there.

MEASURES OF DISTRIBUTIONAL EQUALITY

The reduction of disparities in the distribution of per-pupil revenues (or expenditures) has been one of the principal objectives of the reform movement. There is conceptual appeal in the other objectives—reducing disparities in the cost-adjusted or the pupil-need-adjusted distribution of per-pupil revenues (or expenditures)—but we presently have neither cost-of-education indexes nor the methods and data for constructing them. Nor do we have the means for assessing pupils' needs in ways that translate into revenue or expenditure requirements. Accordingly, this analysis focuses on the degree to which reform has brought about greater equality in per-pupil spending or receipts.

We use two measures of the degree of distributional equality achieved by a state's school finance system: the *coefficient of variation* and the *relative deviation from the median*. The former is the standard deviation divided by the mean; the latter is the average (mean) absolute deviation from the median divided by the median.

The coefficient of variation can be intuitively interpreted as follows: A value of, say, 0.20 means that about one-sixth of the students are in districts where revenues (instructional expenditures, tax rates) are 20 percent or more above the mean, and about one-sixth where they are at least 20 percent below the mean. Roughly two-thirds of the students are in districts where the variable of interest is within 20 percent of the mean. The relative deviation from the median equals half the difference between the average revenues (instructional expenditures, tax rates) for pupils above the median and the average revenues for below-median pupils, expressed as a percentage of the median. It is thus the percentage by which statewide per-pupil revenues would have to be increased to raise all below-median pupils' revenues to the average achieved by pupils above the median. A relative deviation from the median of, say, 0.20 means that above-median pupils average 40 percent greater revenues than below-median pupils; or, the cost of raising all below-median pupils to the average revenues of above-median pupils would be 20 percent of the statewide average per-pupil revenues. Reductions in either measure signal a move toward greater equality.

Previous studies have used several other measures to summarize the distributional effects of a school finance plan.[8] Many of these measures are redundant in that they provide essentially the same information as that provided by the coefficient of variation and relative deviation from the median. Nonetheless, participants in the reform debate and researchers interested in the consequences of school finance plans seem to find different measures useful. To facilitate comparison of our results with those obtained in other studies, and to serve the purposes of readers familiar with different measures, we computed most of the other distributional measures that have appeared in the literature; Carroll (1979) provides the following measures for each state for each year, both unweighted and weighted by district size:

Percentiles. We ranked the districts according to the variable of interest and listed the value of the variable for the 100th (highest), 95th, 75th, 50th (median), 25th, 5th, and 1st (lowest) percentile district. When the percentile fell between two districts, we used the average of their values.

Range. The difference between the values of a variable in the highest and the lowest districts.

Restricted range. The difference between the values of a variable at the 95th and the 5th percentile. The measure is also known as the federal range ratio. It is the number of times the variable at the 95th percentile is larger than at the 5th percentile.

Mean deviation from the median. The average (mean) absolute deviation from the median divided by the median.

Mean. The sum of the values of the variable over the districts divided by the number of districts.

Standard deviation. The square root of the sum of the squared differences between the value of the variable in each district and the mean, divided by the number of districts minus one.

Coefficient of variation. The standard deviation divided by the mean.

[8]Berne (1978) analyzes numerous measures of expenditure equality and fiscal neutrality.

Mean deviation from mean. The average (mean) absolute deviation between the value of the variable in each district and the mean.

Relative mean deviation from the mean. The mean absolute deviation from the mean divided by the mean.

Gini coefficient. A Lorenz curve shows the cumulative proportion of the aggregate value of a variable plotted against the cumulative proportion of districts, when districts are ranked in ascending order by the variable. It is a straight line, with a positive 45-degree slope, bisecting a unit square, if the variable has the same value in every district. If the variable is not equally distributed across districts, the curve will "sag" below the 45-degree line. The Gini coefficient is one-half the area between the Lorenz curve and the 45-degree line.

MEASURES OF FISCAL NEUTRALITY

The school finance reform movement grew out of a concern for the distribution of revenues or spending among children of various income levels. It was believed that most poor children received fewer school resources than did children from higher income families, mainly because they lived in low-value housing in districts that consequently had low property tax bases. Reform efforts therefore focused on eliminating the link between a district's revenues and its property tax base. The California Supreme Court, in the *Serrano* decision, accepted the argument and interpreted it as requiring that there be no correlation between the two. This notion of fiscal neutrality is now generally accepted.

Meanwhile, research has shown that, in many states, surprising numbers of poor children do not live in property-poor districts. Commercial and industrial property accounts for a large share of many districts' tax base; this is particularly true of the central-city districts. And poor families are more likely than higher income families to live near commercial centers and industrial facilities and in the central cities. For that reason, reforms that break the link between a district's revenues and its property tax base generally will not improve the relative condition of poor children. That is not to say such reforms are meaningless or irrelevant, but they fail to address the issue of the degree to which a district's revenues depend on the income level of the population it serves.

The distinction between ex ante and ex post wealth neutrality is also troublesome. Feldstein (1975) has shown that an ex ante fiscally neutral system will not, in general, yield ex post fiscal neutrality. Finance systems which guarantee that districts' revenues will depend only on their fiscal efforts will generally result in districts' revenues being correlated with their tax bases. And finance systems that achieve ex post fiscal neutrality (i.e., a negligible correlation between districts' revenues and tax bases) must offer different rewards to districts that exert similar efforts.

Against this background, we explore the effects of each state's reform on three different concepts of fiscal neutrality. The first corresponds to the currently popular notion that fiscal neutrality requires ex post independence between districts' revenues or expenditures and their property tax bases. We regress each of the variables of interest (the per-pupil revenue measures, instructional expenditures per pupil, and the adjusted tax rate) on the adjusted (to market value) property tax base per pupil and the square of the adjusted property tax base per pupil. We use the implied elasticity of the variable with respect to wealth (calculated at the mean) as the indicator of the magnitude to which the variable of interest is associated with a district's wealth.

Second, we regress each variable of interest on per-pupil income (of the population served by the district) and the square of household income per pupil. The implied elasticity indicates the magnitude of the relationship between the variable and per-pupil household income. This part of the analysis responds to the concerns that originally motivated reform efforts.

Finally, to explore the ex ante fiscal neutrality of a state's finance plan, we regress each variable of interest (except the adjusted tax rate) on the adjusted tax rate and the adjusted tax rate squared. If we accept the adjusted tax rate as a measure of fiscal effort, a greater magnitude of association between a revenue or expenditure variable and (the quadratic form of) the adjusted tax rate implies a more ex ante fiscally neutral system. The elasticities of these regressions indicate the extent to which a district's revenues or expenditures depend on its effort.

We also computed several other measures of fiscal neutrality that have been used in other studies. Carroll (1979) provides the following measures, unweighted and weighted by districts' sizes, for each state in each year:

Regression on adjusted wealth. We regress the variable of interest on assessed value per pupil (in thousands) adjusted to market value per pupil. (We use the same factor for each district that was used to adjust its expressed property tax rate to the effective rate levied on the market value of property.) We also regress the variable on adjusted wealth per pupil and adjusted wealth per pupil squared.[9] We obtain two measures of fiscal neutrality from each regression: The *F*-statistic for the regression is an indicator of "goodness-of-fit"—the degree to which the variable is related to adjusted value. A higher *F*-statistic indicates a higher probability that the observed relationship between the variable, the adjusted per-pupil wealth, is nonrandom. The elasticity shows the nature of the estimated relationship between the variable and adjusted wealth per pupil. It is the estimated percentage change in the variable that, at the mean, is associated with a 1 percent change in adjusted per-pupil wealth.

Regression on income. We regress the variable of interest on household income per pupil and on household income per pupil squared, and obtain the *F*-statistic and elasticity at the mean for each regression.

Regression on adjusted tax rate. We regress the variable of interest on the adjusted tax rate and on the adjusted tax rate squared, and obtain the *F*-statistic and elasticity at the mean for each regression.

Mean for adjusted wealth decile. The districts are ranked by adjusted wealth per pupil and divided into deciles. We compute the mean of the variable of interest for the districts in each decile.

Mean for income decile. We rank the districts by per-pupil household income, divide them into deciles, and compute the mean of the variable of interest for the districts in each decile.

Correlations. We compute the simple correlation between each variable of interest and adjusted per-pupil wealth, household income per pupil, and the adjusted tax rate.

Gini by adjusted wealth distribution. The Gini coefficient for the Lorenz curve obtained by plotting the cumulative value of a variable of interest against the cumulative adjusted wealth per pupil. Districts are ranked in ascending order by the variable of interest per adjusted wealth per pupil and the cumulative value of the variable.

---

[9]We also tried a cubic regression of the variation on adjusted wealth, but we dropped the exercise because, in some cases, the results seemed unduly sensitive to extreme values.

Gini by income distribution. The Gini coefficient for the Lorenz curve obtained by plotting the cumulative value of the variable of interest against cumulative household income per pupil. Districts are ranked in ascending order by the ratio of the variable to household income per pupil.

WINNERS AND LOSERS

If reform means to reshape the distribution of revenues or expenditures among a state's districts, some districts must receive disproportionately large increases (or decreases) in their revenues. Whether one type of district is a winner or loser is not itself a reform issue; but policymakers' and citizens' expectations regarding a reform's likely winners and losers certainly affect the evaluation of the reform and willingness to support it. Furthermore, the unanticipated consequences of reform for certain types of districts may be important. For these reasons, we explored the effects of reform on various types of districts.

Previous studies and policy debates suggested many categories of districts that appear to be of special concern, but we often lacked the data for thus categorizing the districts in our five states. We eventually settled on four district characteristics that seemed to be of policy concern and for which we had data: size, percentage of the district's population residing in urban areas, percentage of the district's population who are white, and percentage of the district's population whose household incomes are below the poverty level. In each case, we ranked the students (weighted districts) in a state according to their district's characteristic and computed the means for each variable of interest for the students below and above the median on that characteristic. We used the ratio of the mean for the below-median students to the mean for the above-median students as an indicator of the way students living in various types of districts fared under their state's finance system.

Suppose, for example, that we are considering the percentage-urban characteristic, and that in some state the ratio of mean general revenue per pupil between students below and above the median for that characteristic is 0.92. This means that the lower half of the state's students, ranked by their districts' percentage urban, receive about 92 percent as much general revenue as the upper half. The state's finance plan is favoring the more urban districts. If that ratio pertained to a prereform year but rose to 0.95 after reform, we would infer that the gap had narrowed.

The unweighted counterpart of that ratio is obtained by dividing districts, unweighted, at the median of a district characteristic, and taking the ratio of the unweighted mean for the above-median districts to the unweighted mean for the below-median districts.

Carroll (1979) presents the unweighted (weighted) means for each variable of interest in each state in each year for districts (students) above and below the median on each variable of interest and each characteristic.

DATA

We obtained data from state sources on districts' revenues, tax rates, wealth, and number of pupils. These data are described in the state-by-state discussions below. Data on household income, percentage urban, percentage white, and percentage poverty-prone were obtained from 1970 census fifth-count information compiled to 1974 school district boundaries. We use the census definitions of household income, urbanization, race, and poverty level.

In computing any measure for any variable, we include all the districts in a state for which data were available. The measures pertaining to the distributions of the variables of interest or to the relationships between them and size, adjusted wealth, or adjusted tax rates are generally computed over every district in the state. In a few cases, however, the data required for calculating one or another of our variables for a district were missing in some year, or were clearly erroneous and correct information could not be obtained. That district is dropped in calculating the measures for that variable in that year. It is included, however, in calculating the measures of other variables (if the data were available) in that year and of that variable (if the data were available) in other years.

The measures relating our variables to income, urbanization, race, and poverty are computed over all districts that could be matched to the census data. Because the census data were not compiled for districts serving fewer than 300 pupils in 1970, small districts are generally excluded from measures relating variables to census data. There were also a few larger districts in each state that could not be matched to the census file. They, too, were dropped in computing the measures involving income, urbanization, race, and poverty.

Districts that consolidated were treated as independent entities prior to their merger and as a single entity thereafter. We made no attempts to "create" consolidated districts in premerger years or to partition consolidated districts after their merger.

4 THE EFFECTS OF REFORM IN CALIFORNIA

Because California's finance systems, both before and after reform, treat elementary, high school, and unified districts differently, we separately examine the effects of reform on each type of district. In each case we examine how reform affected the distribution of revenues per pupil, instructional expenditures per pupil, and adjusted tax rates; reform's contribution to fiscal neutrality; and the benefits and losses that various kinds of districts experienced. The chapter ends with our conclusions regarding the effects of reform in California.

SCHOOL FINANCE IN CALIFORNIA

The California school finance reform was passed late in 1972 and modified in the summer of 1973, just before it took effect. It was part of a larger reform package (Senate Bill 90) affecting all local governments. For school districts, reform basically amounted to a substantial increase in the foundation programs coupled with the imposition of revenue limits. The state attempted to equalize districts' general revenues by increasing state support and by limiting revenue growth in the high-spending districts so that lower spending districts could catch up.

The Prereform System

Prior to reform, California provided general support to the schools through three programs. The basic aid program provided flat grants of

$125 per pupil to every district, based on average daily attendance (ADA). [1] Equalization aid was distributed through a foundation program. Most districts were guaranteed $335 per elementary ADA and $488 per high school ADA. [2] An additional $30 was paid per primary (grades 1–3) ADA. Finally, supplemental support of $125 per ADA less 1 percent of assessed value was provided to districts where the assessed valuation was less than $12,500 per ADA.

To encourage "more efficient organization of schools" (meaning unification), a $20 per ADA unification bonus was included in the foundation program. It was paid to unified districts and to districts that voted favorably in an unsuccessful unification election.

The required foundation program participation tax and the foundation program aid were administered on an area-wide basis. A property-poor district could thus find itself ineligible for equalization aid if it had the ill luck to be located in a property-rich area. If the area as a whole qualified for equalization aid, the amount of the area-wide tax (the foundation program minimum tax) allocated to each district was proportional to its share of the area's total foundation program. Equalization aid distributed to districts was, then, the difference between the district's foundation program and its receipts from basic aid and its share of the area-wide tax. [3]

Inflation factor adjustments were included in 1970, 1971, and 1972. These provided additional funds, for school cost increases, to be distributed to all districts receiving equalization aid. Districts received a share of the additional funds in proportion to their share of the statewide equalized ADA.

The Postreform System

The reform package left the basic aid program unchanged. It boosted foundation support to $909 per elementary ADA and $1,094 per high

---

[1] Districts with an ADA of nineteen or less were guaranteed a minimum basic aid of $2,400. There were thirty-six such elementary districts in 1972–73.

[2] For the smallest elementary schools (under 101 ADA but "necessary"), the amount of foundation support was related to the student-teacher ratio. For small school districts not determined to be "necessary," the foundation support level was reduced by $10 per ADA because the districts were eligible for certain services at no cost from the county.

[3] In the 1972–73 school year, 329 districts, of which 5 had an ADA of nineteen or less, received only basic aid. These were primarily small elementary districts in the state's rural areas.

school ADA, and repealed supplemental aid for districts with low assessed value per ADA. The unification bonus and support for "necessary" small schools was retained. [4]

To hold down increases in school expenditures, Senate Bill 90 established revenue limits that were based on the previous year's revenue per ADA, adjusted for inflation. Each year, each district is allowed to increase its noncategorical revenues per ADA by an amount specified by the legislature times its "squeeze factor." A district's squeeze factor is the year's revenue limit.

Each district's revenue limit was translated into a maximum general-purpose tax rate (basic aid and equalization aid are subtracted from the revenue limit and result divided by assessed valuation). A district can levy a higher general-purpose tax rate only with the approval of the electorate. Tax override porposals have to specify the time period during which the override will hold; that period can be extended only with voter approval.

Aside from the systems for providing general support to school districts, California has a system of state support for pupil-targed instructional programs, pupil support services, and capital expenditures. The pupil-targeted instructional programs include special funds over and above the foundation program for physically handicapped, mentally retarded, educationally handicapped, and mentally gifted minors. The state assists districts in the behind-the-wheel driver training program. The educationally disadvantaged youth program gives districts additional funds for programs for poor, transient, and non-English-speaking students on a need basis. The state provides funds for a home-to-school transportation to districts up to the level of the median expense statewide.

The immediate impact of reform was a large increase in the state's share of total school revenues. In the 1973–74 school year, the first affected by reform, the state share of total income was 42 percent, a one-third increase over the 31 percent share the year before. In succeeding years, however, state funds have barely kept pace with the rate of growth in districts' total revenues. Table 4–1 provides summary data on California school districts and their revenues by source for the 1970–71 through 1976–77 school years.

[4]A total of 486 school districts received only basic aid in the first year of reform. For the most part, these were the same small, rural, elementary districts that had received only basic aid in the year immediately prior to reform. The rest were smaller districts (many serving fewer than 100 pupils) that had sizable enrollment changes.

Table 4–1. Summary Data on California Elementary, High School, and Unified Districts (dollar amounts in millions).

Type of District	1970–71	1971–72	1972–73	1973–74	1974–75	1975–76	1976–77
All districts							
Number of districts	1,322	1,326	1,328	1,296	1,270	1,246	1,227
Assessed valuation ($)	55,289	58,529	62,474	66,839	73,785	81,858	92,557
Average daily attendance	4,692,295	4,664,034	4,629,135	4,612,621	4,665,615	4,699,266	4,666,780
Revenue							
Federal	225	318	337	318	392	359	427
Combined federal and state	9	9	12	10	8	15	8
State	1,478	1,462	1,536	2,262	2,420	2,689	2,850
County	25	29	34	54	49	43	51
Local	2,364	2,623	3,000	2,780	3,062	3,459	3,872
Total, all sources	4,132	4,441	4,981	5,424	5,931	6,603	7,254
Elementary districts							
Number of districts	917	920	918	884	860	835	828
Assessed valuation ($)	17,488	18,614	20,060	20,943	23,451	29,163	29,080
Average daily attendance	1,082,396	1,062,811	1,051,895	1,010,025	983,246	978,328	952,046
Revenue							
Federal	49	60	63	62	75	80	87
Combined federal and state	3	3	4	4	3	3	3
State	350	332	360	515	528	581	623
County	5	6	7	12	11	9	11
Local	458	503	558	526	571	651	715
Total, all sources	865	904	992	1,118	1,188	1,325	1,438

High school districts

Number of districts	165	164	165	161	157	154	151
Assessed valuation ($)	17,480	18,605	20,051	20,931	23,438	26,151	29,067
Average daily attendance	525,444	533,965	542,612	544,403	559,589	577,505	579,733
Revenue							
Federal	26	30	31	31	36	40	45
Combined federal and state	0	1	0	1	0	0	0
State	161	160	175	255	262	296	324
County	4	5	6	9	8	8	10
Local	357	393	442	406	444	506	558
Total, all sources	548	588	654	702	750	850	936

Unified districts

Number of districts	240	242	245	251	253	254	258
Assessed valuation ($)	37,802	39,915	42,414	45,896	50,335	55,695	63,477
Average daily attendance	3,084,455	3,067,358	3,034,628	3,058,193	3,122,780	3,143,433	3,135,001
Revenue							
Federal	180	228	244	224	281	279	295
Combined federal and state	6	6	8	6	5	12	5
State	967	970	1,000	1,492	1,630	1,811	1,949
County	16	19	21	34	30	27	31
Local	1,549	1,726	2,000	1,847	2,047	2,300	2,599
Total, all sources	2,719	2,948	3,273	3,604	3,993	4,428	4,878

DATA AND DEFINITIONS

We obtained data on California districts' sizes (ADA), assessed values, tax rates, expenditures by category, and revenues by source from the *Fiscal Transactions* files maintained by the Bureau of School Apportionments, California State Department of Education. The information is provided by school districts in annual reports (J-41) to the bureau. The available files covered the 1970–71 through 1976–77 school years. The bureau also provided modified assessed values for each district for the 1971–72 through 1974–75 school years. These are assessed values adjusted to equalize assessment ratios across counties. The State Assessor's Office develops the adjustment factors in annual special studies of county assessment ratios. We use the modified assessed values in 1971–72 through 1974–75, and the unmodified assessed values in 1970–71, 1975–76, and 1976–77.

California assesses all property at 25 percent of fair market value. We divided nominal tax rates, and multiplied assessed values, by 4 to convert them to effective tax rates and market values.

Table 4–2 shows, for each year, the numbers of California districts and students for which we had only finance data and the numbers of each for which we had both finance and census data.

General revenues per pupil is the sum of all local, county, and state noncategorical revenues. It includes basic aid, equalization aid, the unification bonus, support for necessary small schools, the bonus for primary ADA (grades 1–3) and, in the prereform years, supplementary support for districts with low assessed value per pupil. The other revenue variables are self-explanatory. Prior to 1974–75, the schools' accounting system included an instructional expenditure category. The category was eliminated when the accounting system was revised in 1974–75. We used the categorical total for the first four years and, for the last three, estimated instructional expenditures by aggregating the detailed accounts that had been included in the expenditure category in the old system.

California's prereform and postreform plans specify different foundation levels for elementary, high school, and unified districts. The parameters used to calculate revenue limits also vary by district type.

Table 4–2. Numbers of California Districts and Students.

Year and Type of District	Finance Data Available[a]		Finance and Census Data Available	
	No. of Districts[b]	No. of Students	No. of Districts	No. of Students
Elementary				
1970–71	711	1,082,396	366	1,009,363
1971–72	707	1,062,811	364	987,547
1972–73	705	1,051,895	364	974,360
1973–74	687	1,010,025	364	961,191
1974–75	678	981,355	359	931,627
1975–76	676	978,328	359	927,389
1976–77	669	952,046	356	900,147
High School				
1970–71	118	525,444	107	511,768
1971–72	117	533,965	107	522,960
1972–73	117	542,612	107	530,468
1973–74	114	544,403	106	542,586
1974–75	114	559,589	106	557,711
1975–76	114	577,505	106	575,494
1976–77	115	579,733	106	577,209
Unified				
1970–71	240	3,084,455	227	3,057,119
1971–72	242	3,066,881	228	3,035,359
1972–73	244	3,034,628	232	3,007,277
1973–74	251	3,058,193	238	3,022,392
1974–75	248	3,095,609	234	3,031,062
1975–76	254	3,143,433	238	3,075,720
1976–77	258	3,135,001	238	3,055,590

[a]Finance data are available for all districts and students in all years with the following exceptions: One high school district serving 377 students is missing in 1971 and five unified districts serving 27,171 students are missing in 1974.

[b]California's unification procedure occasionally results in "operating" districts that have no students; such districts are excluded.

In essence, California operates three different school finance systems, one for each type of district. We separately analyze the effects of reform for each type of district.

ELEMENTARY SCHOOL DISTRICTS

The Distribution of Revenues, Instructional Expenditures, and Adjusted Tax Rates

Table 4–3 presents our data on elementary districts.

Table 4–3. Measures of the Distribution of Revenues, Instructional Expenditures, and Adjusted Tax Rates: California Elementary Districts, 1970–76.

Measure	1970–71	1971–72	1972–73	1973–74	1974–75	1975–76	1976–77
General revenue							
Mean	729	763	845	984	1,060	1,181	1,308
Coefficient of variation	0.23	0.24	0.22	0.21	0.20	0.19	0.18
Median	681	717	800	930	983	1,115	1,254
Relative deviation	0.16	0.17	0.15	0.14	0.14	0.13	0.12
General + PL 874 revenue							
Mean	745	780	860	999	1,076	1,196	1,327
Coefficient of variation	0.22	0.23	0.22	0.21	0.20	0.18	0.18
Median	701	732	812	941	996	1,129	1,258
Relative deviation	0.15	0.16	0.15	0.14	0.14	0.13	0.12
Local + state revenue							
Mean	778	818	907	1,072	1,169	1,310	1,463
Coefficient of variation	0.22	0.23	0.22	0.20	0.19	0.17	0.16
Median	730	774	856	1,008	1,097	1,267	1,411
Relative deviation	0.15	0.16	0.15	0.14	0.13	0.12	0.12

Local + state + PL 874 revenue

Mean	794	835	923	1,087	1,185	1,325	1,482
Coefficient of variation	0.21	0.22	0.21	0.20	0.18	0.17	0.16
Median	745	797	874	1,018	1,111	1,276	1,442
Relative deviation	0.15	0.15	0.15	0.14	0.13	0.12	0.11
Total revenue							
Mean	832	886	982	1,151	1,268	1,420	1,586
Coefficient of variation	0.20	0.20	0.20	0.19	0.18	0.17	0.16
Median	803	848	932	1,097	1,218	1,386	1,554
Relative deviation	0.13	0.14	0.14	0.14	0.13	0.12	0.11
Instructional expenditures							
Mean	553	591	634	717	684	746	821
Coefficient of variation	0.17	0.17	0.17	0.16	0.18	0.16	0.15
Median	545	576	613	699	663	728	798
Relative deviation	0.12	0.12	0.13	0.12	0.12	0.11	0.11
Adjusted tax rates							
Mean	7.2	7.4	7.6	6.7	6.7	7.0	6.9
Coefficient of variation	0.22	0.23	0.23	0.22	0.17	0.17	0.17
Median	7.0	7.3	7.8	6.6	6.7	6.8	6.7
Relative deviation	0.19	0.19	0.19	0.17	0.13	0.13	0.13

Note: All revenue measures and instructional expenditures are dollars per pupil. Adjusted tax rates are mills.

General Revenues per Pupil.   General revenues per pupil increased by 80 percent between 1970 and 1976, and the coefficient of variation began a continuous although slow decline with the introduction of reform in 1973. (The reader will recall that a decrease in the coefficient of variation is a movement toward equality.) The relative deviation from the median has also declined. Reform has reduced disparities in general revenues per pupil.

General Plus PL 874 Revenues Per Pupil.   Public Law 874 revenues averaged $15 to $20 per pupil in each year between 1970 and 1976. Funding from this program had a slightly equalizing effect in 1970 and 1971, when both the coefficient of variation and relative deviation from the median were lower than they were for general revenues per pupil. Since then, however, PL 874 revenues have not affected the distribution of revenues per pupil.

Local Plus State Revenues Per Pupil.   Local plus state revenues per pupil equals the sum of general revenues per pupil and state categorical revenues per pupil. Consequently, the difference between the two variables in Table 4–3 reveal the effects of categorical programs. These programs more than tripled between 1970 and 1976—from $50 to about $155 per pupil—and since reform have had an equalizing effect on the distribution of revenues among pupils.

Local Plus State Plus PL 874 Revenues Per Pupil.   PL 874 revenues per pupil have not substantially affected the distribution of revenues among pupils.

Total Revenues Per Pupil.   Total revenues per pupil is obtained by adding federal categorical revenues per pupil to local plus state plus PL 874 revenues per pupil. Federal categorical revenues have been substantial: about $40 per pupil in 1970, growing to over $100 by 1976. Their distribution appears to have had a slight equalizing effect before reform, but almost none afterward.

The aggregate effect of categorical programs, both federal and state, is suggested by comparing the results shown for general plus PL 874 revenues per pupil and for total revenues per pupil. The former includes general aid revenues from all sources; the latter, both general aid from all sources and categorical revenues from all sources. In principle, categorical programs are designed to provide additional funds to selected categories of students (e.g., more expensive-to-educate students or students engaged in more expensive programs). No such public purpose is served by inequalities in general revenues per pupil. Accordingly, one would expect greater equality in the distribution of general plus PL 874 revenues per pupil than in the distribution of total revenues per pupil. In California elementary districts, however, we see precisely the reverse result. Both before and after reform, the coefficient of variation for general plus PL 874 revenues per pupil is about 10 percent greater than for total revenues per pupil. Approximately the same relation holds in comparing the relative deviation from the median for two variables in any given year, though the differences between them are not as dramatic in the postreform years. In other words, state and federal categorical programs seem to be distributing funds in a way that reduces disparities in general revenues per pupil.

Instructional Expenditures Per Pupil.   Before reform, instructional expenditures per pupil were more equally distributed than were revenues per pupil. Reform has slightly reduced disparities in instructional expenditures per pupil. The coefficients of variation are a point or two lower in postreform years, and the relative deviation from the median has also decreased.

It is interesting to note that both the coefficients of variation and the relative deviations from the median for the distributions of instructional expenditures per pupil are smaller than those for the distributions of revenues per pupil. Higher revenue districts apparently allocate a large share of their funds to noninstructional purposes. Furthermore, when variation in per-pupil revenues declined, the variation in the instructional expenditures declined less. This suggests that when reform substantially increased a low-spending district's revenues, it tended to put its newfound funds to noninstructional uses. These results are consistent with those of previous studies (Alexander 1974; Barro and Carroll 1975; Carroll 1976), which found that as districts' per-pupil budgets increase, they spend proportionately less on teachers.

Taken together, these observations suggest the following hypothesis: School districts generally agree on what constitutes an acceptable instructional program and exert every effort to provide one. In doing so, low-revenue-per-pupil districts make do with meager noninstructional resources. Wealthier districts provide a somewhat better instructional program, but spend much more money on noninstructional resources. When a poorer district's budget is increased, it spends somewhat more on teachers, but much more on "catching up" on non-instructional resources.

Adjusted Tax Rates.   Adjusted tax rates, which had been growing at a rate of about 0.2 mills per year before reform, dropped sharply with reform. At the same time, reform has promoted greater equality in the distribution of adjusted tax rates. Both distributional measures were roughly constant prior to reform, dipped in the first year of reform, and then dropped more sharply.

Wealth, Income, and Tax Neutrality

Table 4–4 shows the elasticity (at the mean) for each variable of interest. The elasticity measure indicates the percentage change in the variable that, on average, is associated with a 1 percent change in wealth, income, or tax rates.

Revenues Per Pupil.   The elasticity of each revenue measure with respect to wealth declined in the postreform years. The percentage increase in per-pupil revenues associated with a 1 percent increase in wealth fell by about one-third between 1972, the last prereform year, and 1976. The same pattern holds true for household income; revenue elasticity diminished 30 percent between 1972 and 1976. In general, reform has substantially improved the ex post wealth neutrality and income neutrality of revenue distributions among elementary districts.

The elasticity of revenues with respect to the adjusted tax rate jumped sharply in the first two reform years, but then fell back to prereform levels in 1975 and 1976. A district's tax effort is no more closely associated with its per-pupil revenues after reform than it had been before. There is no improvement in ex ante fiscal neutrality.

Instructional Expenditures Per Pupil.   Reform has had little effect on the relationship between instructional expenditures per pupil and either wealth or income. And the elasticity of per-pupil instructional expenditures with respect to the tax rate was dramatically lower in the last two years, 1975 and 1976, than it had been before reform. Among elementary districts, reform has not improved the wealth or income neutrality of instructional expenditures and has very much worsened that variable's ex ante fiscal neutrality.

Table 4—4. Elasticity of Revenues, Instructional Expenditures, and Adjusted Tax Rates with Respect to Adjusted Wealth, Household Income, and Adjusted Tax Rates: California Elementary Districts, 1970–76.

Dependent/Independent Variable	*1970–71*	*1971–72*	*1972–73*	*1973–74*	*1974–75*	*1975–76*	*1976–77*
General revenue							
Adjusted wealth	0.210	0.229	0.225	0.212	0.188	0.156	0.154
Household income	0.210	0.216	0.210	0.207	0.196	0.170	0.158
Adjusted tax rate	0.238	0.211	0.199	0.492	0.457	0.222	0.215
General + PL 874 revenue							
Adjusted wealth	0.195	0.214	0.214	0.202	0.180	0.150	0.148
Household income	0.197	0.199	0.198	0.197	0.185	0.160	0.149
Adjusted tax rate	0.167	0.138	0.135	0.434	0.385	0.159	0.138
Local + state revenue							
Adjusted wealth	0.195	0.213	0.208	0.188	0.164	0.136	0.131
Household income	0.198	0.205	0.199	0.187	0.170	0.149	0.140
Adjusted tax rate	0.243	0.214	0.208	0.472	0.457	0.240	0.227
Local + state + PL 874 revenue							
Adjusted wealth	0.182	0.199	0.198	0.180	0.157	0.131	0.126
Household income	0.186	0.190	0.187	0.177	0.161	0.141	0.133
Adjusted tax rate	0.176	0.147	0.148	0.418	0.392	0.183	0.158
Total revenue							
Adjusted wealth	0.166	0.177	0.175	0.159	0.138	0.112	0.110
Household income	0.160	0.157	0.154	0.149	0.129	0.111	0.108
Adjusted tax rate	0.139	0.113	0.124	0.383	0.378	0.175	0.144
Instructional expenditures							
Adjusted wealth	0.096	0.105	0.108	0.090	0.117	0.101	0.104
Household income	0.145	0.146	0.152	0.135	0.136	0.126	0.124
Adjusted tax rate	0.259	0.235	0.257	0.422	0.300	0.073	0.029
Adjusted tax rates							
Adjusted wealth	−0.082	−0.098	−0.114	0.021	−0.024	−0.060	−0.065
Household income	−0.004	−0.021	−0.026	0.122	0.068	0.004	−0.012

Adjusted Tax Rates.   Before reform, the elasticity of the adjusted tax rate with respect to adjusted wealth per pupil was about -0.1. Wealthier districts enjoyed lower property tax rates, and a 1 percent increase in wealth per pupil was associated at the mean with a decrease of about 0.1 percent in the adjusted tax rate. Reform reduced the dependence of wealth per pupil on adjusted tax rates. Household income had been negatively related to the adjusted tax rates prior to reform. The elasticity of the adjusted tax rate with respect to household income per pupil is positive in the first three reform years, suggesting that school districts serving relatively higher income populations were levying somewhat higher local property taxes for educational purposes in those years. By 1976, however, the elasticity became negative once again.

Winners and Losers

Table 4–5 shows the effects of reform on the distributions of revenues per pupil, instructional expenditures per pupil, and adjusted tax rates among various types of elementary districts.

Revenues Per Pupil.   In terms of general revenues per pupil:
- The more poverty-prone districts have been the bigger winners. Before reform, the wealthier districts enjoyed about 17 to 19 percent more general revenue per pupil. Reform cut their advantage to 10 percent. And with respect to total revenues per pupil, the reduction was dramatic: In 1976, the wealthier districts received about 1 percent *less* per pupil than the more poverty-prone districts.
- Both before and after reform, the smaller districts received 3 to 7 percent more general revenues per pupil than the larger ones.
- The more urban districts' 9 percent advantage over the less urban before reform dropped to 6 percent in 1975 and 1976.
- The distributions between the more white and more minority districts were fairly equal both before and after reform.

The results for the other revenue measures are similar: The smaller districts had greater revenue per pupil before reform, and their advantage over the larger districts grew slightly with reform. The less urban districts had lower revenue per pupil by each measure than the more urban, but they caught up slightly with reform. Reform has not substantially affected the distribution of revenues between the more white and the more minority districts on any revenue measure.

Instructional Expenditures Per Pupil. The more white districts gained about 5 percentage points on the more minority districts; otherwise, reform has had little effect on the distribution of instructional expenditures per pupil among various kinds of districts. The smaller and less urban districts made only modest gains on their larger and more urban counterparts. The distribution has shifted slightly in favor of the less poverty-prone districts.

Adjusted Tax Rates. Reform has equalized the distribution of adjusted tax rates among various types of districts. Before reform, small districts enjoyed tax rates that were only 84 to 86 percent of those in the larger districts; the figure rose to 90 percent by 1976. A similiar pattern holds for less urban districts. The less poverty-prone districts levied tax rates about 16 to 17 percent higher than those in the more poverty-prone districts before reform. Reform reduced that figure; in 1976, the rates were only about 5 percent higher.

HIGH SCHOOL DISTRICTS

The Distribution of Revenues, Instructional Expenditures, and Adjusted Tax Rates

Table 4–6 presents data on high school districts.

General Revenues Per Pupil. General revenues per pupil grew less rapidly between 1970 and 1976 than they did in elementary school districts: 52 percent versus 80 percent. Reform has slightly reduced disparities in high school districts' per-pupil general revenues, but the coefficient of variation is only a point or two lower in the postreform years. Similarly, by 1976, the relative deviation from the median was only two points below its prereform values.

General Plus PL 874 Revenues Per Pupil. Pl 874 revenues per pupil averaged about $15 in each of the five years. As with elementary districts, these funds have had no effect upon revenue patterns.

Local Plus State Revenues Per Pupil. High school districts have received substantially less revenues per pupil from state categorical pro-

Table 4-5. Distribution of Revenues, Instructional Expenditures, and Adjusted Tax Rates by District Characteristic: California Elementary Districts, 1970–76.

District Characteristic	Ratio of Mean for Students below Median to Mean for Students above Median						
	1970–71	1971–72	1972–73	1973–74	1974–75	1975–76	1976–77
General revenue							
Size	1.03	1.04	1.05	1.04	1.07	1.06	1.04
% urban	0.91	0.92	0.93	0.93	0.95	0.94	0.94
% white	0.99	0.98	1.00	1.00	0.98	1.00	1.01
% poverty	1.17	1.19	1.17	1.11	1.11	1.09	1.10
General + PL 874 revenue							
Size	1.04	1.05	1.06	1.04	1.08	1.07	1.05
% urban	0.93	0.93	0.93	0.94	0.96	0.95	0.96
% white	1.01	1.01	1.02	1.02	1.00	1.01	1.02
% poverty	1.15	1.16	1.15	1.10	1.10	1.08	1.08
Local + state revenue							
Size	1.03	1.04	1.04	1.03	1.07	1.07	1.04
% urban	0.92	0.92	0.92	0.94	0.96	0.96	0.95
% white	0.99	0.98	1.00	1.01	0.99	1.01	1.01
% poverty	1.16	1.17	1.15	1.08	1.07	1.05	1.06

Local + state + PL 874 revenue							
Size	1.03	1.05	1.05	1.04	1.07	1.07	1.05
% urban	0.93	0.93	0.93	0.94	0.97	0.96	0.96
% white	1.01	1.01	1.02	1.03	1.01	1.02	1.03
% poverty	1.14	1.15	1.13	1.06	1.05	1.04	1.04
Total revenue							
Size	1.04	1.06	1.06	1.04	1.08	1.08	1.06
% urban	0.94	0.95	0.95	0.97	0.99	0.98	0.98
% white	1.03	1.02	1.04	1.05	1.04	1.05	1.05
% poverty	1.08	1.08	1.06	1.00	0.98	0.98	0.99
Instructional expenditures							
Size	0.98	0.99	0.98	0.96	1.02	1.01	1.01
% urban	0.93	0.91	0.91	0.92	0.96	0.95	0.94
% white	1.04	1.04	1.04	1.05	1.02	1.02	0.99
% poverty	1.09	1.10	1.11	1.07	1.11	1.12	1.13
Adjusted tax rates							
Size	0.86	0.85	0.84	0.89	0.93	0.91	0.90
% urban	0.88	0.89	0.90	0.90	0.93	0.95	0.95
% white	1.01	1.02	1.02	1.02	1.02	1.04	1.06
% poverty	1.17	1.17	1.16	1.17	1.10	1.07	1.05

Table 4-6. Measures of the Distribution of Revenues, Instructional Expenditures, and Adjusted Tax Rates: California High School Districts, 1970-76.

Measure	1970-71	1971-72	1972-73	1973-74	1974-75	1975-76	1976-77
General revenue							
Mean	990	1,040	1,134	1,214	1,258	1,375	1,505
Coefficient of variation	0.18	0.19	0.18	0.19	0.17	0.17	0.16
Median	964	1,048	1,125	1,243	1,279	1,396	1,535
Relative deviation	0.13	0.13	0.13	0.14	0.13	0.12	0.11
General + PL 874 revenue							
Mean	1,007	1,058	1,148	1,230	1,274	1,388	1,519
Coefficient of variation	0.17	0.18	0.18	0.19	0.17	0.17	0.16
Median	976	1,044	1,138	1,251	1,301	1,397	1,552
Relative deviation	0.12	0.13	0.13	0.14	0.12	0.12	0.11
Local + state revenue							
Mean	1,028	1,080	1,182	1,267	1,370	1,443	1,579
Coefficient of variation	0.18	0.18	0.18	0.18	0.16	0.17	0.15
Median	998	1,054	1,172	1,270	1,327	1,463	1,595
Relative deviation	0.12	0.13	0.13	0.14	0.12	0.12	0.11

Local + state + PL 874 revenue							
Mean	1,044	1,098	1,196	1,283	1,333	1,455	1,594
Coefficient of variation	0.17	0.18	0.17	0.18	0.16	0.17	0.15
Median	1,003	1,075	1,188	1,288	1,351	1,464	1,609
Relative deviation	0.12	0.13	0.12	0.13	0.12	0.12	0.11
Total revenue							
Mean	1,080	1,140	1,244	1,330	1,389	1,521	1,669
Coefficient of variation	0.17	0.17	0.17	0.18	0.16	0.17	0.16
Median	1,040	1,133	1,231	1,348	1,414	1,519	1,677
Relative deviation	0.12	0.12	0.12	0.13	0.12	0.12	0.11
Instructional expenditures							
Mean	723	769	809	869	781	830	899
Coefficient of variation	0.14	0.15	0.15	0.14	0.16	0.15	0.14
Median	697	750	782	851	769	795	887
Relative deviation	0.10	0.11	0.11	0.10	0.12	0.12	0.12
Adjusted tax rates							
Mean	5.6	5.7	6.0	5.3	5.2	5.5	5.4
Coefficient of variation	0.17	0.17	0.17	0.15	0.13	0.14	0.14
Median	5.5	5.7	6.0	5.4	5.3	5.4	5.4
Relative deviation	0.14	0.13	0.14	0.12	0.11	0.11	0.11

Note: All revenue measures and instructional expenditures are dollars per pupil. Adjusted tax rates are mills.

grams than have elementary districts. Comparing local plus state revenues per pupil with general revenues per pupil, we see that state categorical programs accounted for about $38 per pupil in 1970, growing to about $74 in 1974. The coefficient of variation for local plus state revenue per pupil fell by 3 points (about one-sixth) between 1970 and 1976. The relative deviation from the median exhibits even less change.

Total Revenues Per Pupil.   Revenues per pupil from federal categorical programs have grown slowly, from about $36 in 1970 to about $75 in 1974. (Compare total revenues per pupil with local plus state plus PL 874 revenues per pupil.) Federal revenues per pupil have had little effect upon the distribution of total revenues per pupil. We see the familiar pattern of a virtually unchanged distribution of revenues over the 1970 to 1973 period, with some decrease in the coefficient of variation in the 1974 to 1976 period. The relative deviation from the median again shows little change over the five years.

Comparing the results for total revenues per pupil with the results shown for general plus PL 874 revenues per pupil, we see that state and federal categorical programs combined accounted for about $73, or 6 percent, of total revenues in 1970, and grew slowly through 1976, when they accounted for about $150, or 9 percent, of total revenues. The coefficient of variation for total revenues per pupil tends to be about the same as for general plus PL 874 revenues per pupil; similarly, the relative deviation from the median for total revenues per pupil tends to be about the same as for general plus PL 874 revenues per pupil. These results suggest that state and federal categorical programs in California have had no effect on the distribution of general (including PL 874) revenues per pupil.

Instructional Expenditures Per Pupil.   As with elementary districts, both distributional measures for instructional expenditures per pupil tend to be smaller in each year than the corresponding measures for any of the revenue variables. Apparently, districts that obtain relatively large (small) revenues per pupil are devoting disproportionately large (small) shares of those revenues to noninstructional purposes. If anything, reform has widened the disparity in per-pupil instructional expenditures. The coefficient of variation for per-pupil instructional expenditures was not affected by reform. The relative deviation from the median grew from about 0.10 before reform to 0.12 in 1974 through 1976.

Adjusted Tax Rates. Local property taxes for education averaged about 6.0 mills (adjusted to market values) in 1972. Reform produced a sharp decline (about 11 percent) to 5.5 mills in 1976. It was accompanied by a decline in the coefficient of variation from 0.17 in each of the three preform years to 0.13 to 0.14 in subsequent years. The relative deviation from the median exhibits a similar pattern. It appears that reform has lent powerful impetus toward interdistrict equality in local property tax rates for education.

Wealth, Income, and Tax Neutrality

Table 4–7 presents elasticity measures.

Revenues Per Pupil. Reform improved wealth neutrality with regard to general revenues per pupil. The elasticities with respect to adjusted wealth per pupil declined about 25 percent from the preform years to the last postreform years. Nonetheless, general revenues per pupil continue to depend to adjusted wealth per pupil.

A similar, but more dramatic, pattern is evidenced by elasticities of general revenues per pupil with respect to household income per pupil. We observe rough constancy over the preform years, a decline in 1973, and sharp declines in 1974 through 1976. Income neutrality has yet to be achieved, however.

Reform has reversed the relationship between general revenues per pupil in high school districts and local effort, measured by the local property tax rate levied for educational purposes. In 1970 through 1972, general revenues per pupil was negatively associated with adjusted tax rates; districts levying higher taxes tended to have lower general revenues per pupil. Reform initially brought about a large positive elasticity in 1973. Districts levying higher taxes now tended to have higher general revenues per pupil. This elasticity continued to be positive, but declined in value, through 1976.

Similar patterns prevail for the other four revenue measures. In general, the elasticity of revenue per pupil with respect to wealth per pupil was about 25 percent lower following reform.

Household income per pupil is positively related to each revenue measure in all seven years, but the elasticity of each revenue measure with respect to income declined 50 to 60 percent with reform.

Adjusted tax rates were negatively related to each revenue measure in each preform year. As with general revenues per pupil, elasticity with respect to the adjusted tax rate declined through 1976.

Table 4–7. Elasticity of Revenues, Instructional Expenditures, and Adjusted Tax Rates with Respect to Adjusted Wealth, Household Income, and Adjusted Tax Rates: California High School Districts, 1970–76.

Dependent/Independent Variable	1970–71	1971–72	1972–73	1973–74	1974–75	1975–76	1976–77
General revenue							
Adjusted wealth	0.391	0.414	0.404	0.399	0.334	0.332	0.304
Household income	0.286	0.293	0.268	0.276	0.229	0.189	0.136
Adjusted tax rate	−0.176	−0.232	−0.239	0.557	0.398	0.280	0.139
General + PL 874 revenue							
Adjusted wealth	0.380	0.399	0.396	0.388	0.329	0.331	0.307
Household income	0.268	0.274	0.255	0.262	0.219	0.184	0.134
Adjusted tax rate	−0.222	−0.284	−0.275	0.494	0.341	0.232	0.107
Local + state revenue							
Adjusted wealth	0.385	0.402	0.394	0.380	0.321	0.323	0.288
Household income	0.267	0.268	0.238	0.248	0.198	0.164	0.113
Adjusted tax rate	−0.187	−0.237	−0.244	0.516	0.375	0.302	0.139
Local + state + PL 874 revenue							
Adjusted wealth	0.374	0.388	0.386	0.370	0.316	0.321	0.291
Household income	0.250	0.250	0.226	0.235	0.189	0.160	0.112
Adjusted tax rate	−0.231	−0.288	−0.279	0.456	0.321	0.256	0.109
Total revenue							
Adjusted wealth	0.364	0.375	0.372	0.368	0.312	0.313	0.287
Household income	0.212	0.212	0.184	0.201	0.152	0.121	0.078
Adjusted tax rate	−0.253	−0.309	−0.292	0.414	0.270	0.256	0.126
Instructional expenditures							
Adjusted wealth	0.266	0.267	0.286	0.261	0.266	0.268	0.247
Household income	0.153	0.150	0.153	0.115	0.099	0.072	0.077
Adjusted tax rate	−0.057	−0.048	−0.097	0.225	0.070	−0.047	−0.103
Adjusted tax rates							
Adjusted wealth	−0.259	−0.254	−0.283	0.096	−0.018	−0.066	−0.141
Household income	−0.085	−0.071	−0.115	0.179	0.090	0.004	−0.063

In general, the distributions of revenues per pupil among high school districts became more wealth neutral and more income neutral with reform. And reform brought about a more ex ante neutral distribution[5] of per-pupil revenues, in the sense that districts levying higher tax rates obtained greater per-pupil revenue after reform. But the ex ante neutrality of the distributions has consistently declined in the postreform era, undoing some of the improvement obtained in this dimension.

Instructional Expenditures Per Pupil.   Reform appears not to have affected the wealth neutrality of instructional expenditures per pupil in high school districts. The elasticities of instructional expenditures per pupil with respect to adjusted wealth per pupil are about the same as they were before. Household income per pupil, however, has become a much less important predictor of instructional revenues per pupil. Adjusted tax rates are not associated with instructional expenditures per pupil in any year save 1973.

Adjusted Tax Rates.   Reform has sharply reduced the dependence of adjusted tax rates on adjusted wealth per pupil. The elasticity of adjusted tax rates with respect to adjusted wealth was negative in every year except 1973, indicating that higher wealth districts enjoy lower local property tax rates. However, the elasticities are generally lower after reform.

Household income per pupil was negatively related to districts' local property tax rates prior to reform. The elasticity of the adjusted tax rate with respect to household income per pupil is positive since reform. Higher income districts are now levying higher local property taxes for education.

Winners and Losers

Reform has had little effect on the distribution of revenues, instructional expenditures, or adjusted tax rates between large and small districts. Larger districts tended to have somewhat lower revenues per pupil prior to reform, and still do. The advantage of smaller districts increased from about 5 percent before reform to 6 to 8 percent greater average revenues after reform (see Table 4–8.)

[5]See Chapter 3, "Fiscal Neutrality," for an explanation of ex ante and ex post neutrality.

Table 4–8. Distribution of Revenues, Instructional Expenditures, and Adjusted Tax Rates by District Characteristic: California High School Districts, 1970–76.

District Characteristic	Ratio of Mean for Students below Median to Mean for Students above Median						
	1970–71	1971–72	1972–73	1973–74	1974–75	1975–76	1976–77
General revenue							
Size	1.05	1.05	1.10	1.11	1.02	1.06	1.06
% urban	0.95	0.96	0.98	0.99	0.97	1.01	1.01
% white	1.05	1.05	1.04	1.05	1.03	1.04	1.05
% poverty	1.12	1.11	1.10	.08	1.08	1.04	1.03
General + PL 874 revenue							
Size	1.05	1.05	1.10	1.11	1.02	1.07	1.07
% urban	0.96	0.97	0.99	1.00	0.98	1.02	1.02
% white	1.07	1.06	1.05	1.07	1.05	1.05	1.06
% poverty	1.10	1.09	1.09	1.07	1.07	1.03	1.02
Local + state revenue							
Size	1.05	1.05	1.10	1.11	1.02	1.06	1.06
% urban	0.96	0.97	1.00	1.00	0.99	1.03	1.04
% white	1.06	1.05	1.05	1.06	1.04	1.06	1.06
% poverty	1.11	1.10	1.08	1.07	1.06	1.02	1.01

Local + state + PL 874 revenue							
Size	1.05	1.06	1.10	1.11	1.03	1.07	1.07
% urban	0.97	0.98	1.01	1.01	1.00	1.04	1.04
% white	1.07	1.06	1.06	1.07	1.05	1.07	1.07
% poverty	1.09	1.08	1.07	1.05	1.05	1.01	1.00
Total revenue							
Size	1.06	1.07	1.10	1.12	1.04	1.08	1.08
% urban	0.99	1.01	1.03	1.03	1.02	1.07	1.07
% white	1.09	1.08	1.07	1.09	1.07	1.08	1.09
% poverty	1.06	1.05	1.04	1.03	1.01	0.98	0.97
Instructional expenditures							
Size	1.02	1.02	1.05	1.07	1.02	1.05	1.02
% urban	0.99	0.99	0.99	1.02	1.05	1.05	1.05
% white	1.08	1.06	1.06	1.06	1.06	1.10	1.09
% poverty	1.05	1.05	1.06	1.03	1.02	1.00	0.99
Adjusted tax rates							
Size	0.91	0.90	0.88	0.99	0.95	0.98	0.97
% urban	0.98	0.97	1.00	0.99	1.00	1.06	1.01
% white	0.94	0.92	0.91	0.95	0.96	0.98	1.01
% poverty	1.09	1.06	1.06	1.09	1.06	1.00	0.98

Before reform, the less urban districts had average revenues equal to about 95 or 96 percent of those enjoyed by the more urban districts. In general, they gained substantially (6 to 8 percentage points) from reform and now have a 1 to 7 percent advantage over the more urban districts.

The more minority districts had revenues averaging 5 or 6 percent greater than those of more white districts, prior to reform, and have maintained their advantage.

The less poverty-prone districts had revenues 6 to 12 percent greater than those of more poverty-prone districts before reform, but that advantage has generally been eliminated. By 1976, the percentage of a district's population whose incomes were below the poverty level was no longer related to its per-pupil revenues.

For the distribution of instructional expenditures, the less urban districts have gained on the more urban, from 99 percent to 105 percent. More minority districts have retained a roughly 8 percent advantage over the more white districts; and the wealthier districts have lost their advantage over the more poverty-prone.

Reform has substantially equalized adjusted tax rates between the larger and the smaller districts. Tax rates in the smaller districts were formerly about 90 percent of those in the larger districts. By 1976, that figure had risen to 97 percent. The average property tax rate has increased somewhat in the less urban districts and more minority districts, and has declined somewhat in more poverty-prone districts.

UNIFIED SCHOOL DISTRICTS

The Distribution of Revenues, Instructional Expenditures, and Adjusted Tax Rates

Table 4–9 presents data on unified districts.

General Revenues Per Pupil.   General revenues per pupil grew from 7 percent in 1970 to 10 percent per year in 1975 and 1976. Reform substantially reduced disparities in general revenues per pupil. The coefficient of variation fell from 0.19, in the three prereform years, to 0.13 in 1976. The relative deviation from the median also declined sharply.

General Plus PL 874 Revenues Per Pupil.   Impact aid has averaged about $15 per pupil in each of the seven years. These funds have not affected overall revenue patterns among the unified districts.

Local Plus State Revenues Per Pupil.   The districts have enjoyed considerable growth in state categorical programs, from about $50 per pupil in 1970 to $135 in 1974. (Compare local plus state revenues per pupil with general revenues per pupil in each year.) These funds have had little effect on the distributions of revenues among the districts. Year by year, both distributional measures for local plus state revenues are about the same as for general revenues per pupil.

Local Plus State Plus PL 874 Revenues Per Pupil.   PL 874 revenues per pupil have had no discernible effect upon the distribution of revenues at this level of aggregation.

*Total Revenues Per Pupil.*Comparing total revenues per pupil with local plus state plus PL 874 revenues per pupil, we see that revenues from federal categorical aid approximately doubled between 1970 and 1974–from $57 per pupil to $124. Federal categorical revenues seem to have had a slightly disequalizing effect on the unified districts in the postreform years. Both distributional measures are somewhat higher for total revenues than for local plus state plus PL 874 revenues. It appears that federal categorical revenues are disproportionately directed toward those districts whose local plus PL 874 revenues per pupil are relatively high.

Comparing the results for total revenues per pupil with results shown for general plus PL 874 revenues per pupil, we see that state and federal categorical aid combined accounted for about $100 per pupil in the 1970 school year and steadily grew until it accounted for nearly $250 per pupil in the 1976 school year. In all, revenues from categorical programs accounted for about 15 percent of the unified districts' total revenues in 1976. In each of the prereform years the coefficient of variation and the relative deviation from the median for general plus PL 874 revenues were about the same as the comparable measures for total revenues. By 1976, however, both were higher for total revenues than they were for general plus PL 874 revenues. State and federal categorical funds have had a disequalizing effect, then, on the distribution of revenues among unified districts.

Table 4–9. Measures of the Distribution of Revenues, Instructional Expenditures, and Adjusted Tax Rates: California Unified Districts, 1970–76.

Measure	1970–71	1971–72	1972–73	1973–74	1974–75	1975–76	1976–77
General revenue							
Mean	810	866	978	1,062	1,144	1,263	1,393
Coefficient of variation	0.19	0.19	0.19	0.16	0.14	0.14	0.13
Median	783	851	947	1,034	1,113	1,255	1,383
Relative deviation	0.11	0.13	0.15	0.10	0.10	0.08	0.07
General + PL 874 revenue							
Mean	825	882	992	1,078	1,162	1,277	1,412
Coefficient of variation	0.18	0.19	0.18	0.16	0.14	0.14	0.13
Median	790	864	961	1,038	1,170	1,265	1,388
Relative deviation	0.11	0.12	0.14	0.09	0.09	0.08	0.08
Local + state revenue							
Mean	860	925	1,038	1,153	1,246	1,379	1,528
Coefficient of variation	0.19	0.20	0.19	0.16	0.15	0.15	0.13
Median	820	906	1,008	1,130	1,220	1,372	1,530
Relative deviation	0.11	0.12	0.14	0.10	0.10	0.08	0.08

Local + state + PL 874 revenue							
Mean	874	941	1,052	1,169	1,263	1,393	1,546
Coefficient of variation	0.19	0.19	0.18	0.16	0.15	0.14	0.13
Median	827	920	1,017	1,134	1,271	1,384	1,535
Relative deviation	0.11	0.12	0.14	0.09	0.09	0.08	0.08
Total revenue							
Mean	931	1,012	1,135	1,247	1,362	1,502	1,660
Coefficient of variation	0.19	0.19	0.19	0.17	0.16	0.15	0.14
Median	907	988	1,082	1,236	1,358	1,491	1,648
Relative deviation	0.11	0.12	0.15	0.10	0.11	0.10	0.09
Instructional expenditures							
Mean	628	665	712	792	715	757	833
Coefficient of variation	0.17	0.17	0.18	0.17	0.18	0.15	0.13
Median	605	631	697	782	689	718	794
Relative deviation	0.10	0.11	0.10	0.10	0.11	0.09	0.08
Adjusted tax rates							
Mean	11.3	11.8	12.1	11.1	11.6	11.8	11.7
Coefficient of variation	0.17	0.16	0.17	0.15	0.14	0.13	0.12
Median	10.8	11.1	11.5	10.9	11.6	12.0	12.0
Relative deviation	0.13	0.13	0.14	0.10	0.11	0.08	0.08

Note: All revenue measures and instructional expenditures are dollars per pupil. Adjusted tax rates are mills.

Instructional Expenditures Per Pupil.   Both distributional measures for instructional expenditures per pupil declined in 1975 and 1976. As with elementary and high school districts, disparities in instructional expenditures per pupil declined, but slower than disparities in revenues.

Adjusted Tax Rates.   Local property taxes for education in California's unified districts averaged about 12 mills in each of the seven years. While the average level has remained the same, reform has reduced interdistrict disparities in property tax rates. The coefficient of variation fell from its prereform level of about 0.17 to about 0.13, and the relative deviation from the median fell from about 0.13 to about 0.09.

Wealth, Income, and Tax Neutrality

Table 4–10 presents elasticities of revenues per pupil, instructional expenditures per pupil, and adjusted tax rates with respect to adjusted wealth per pupil, household income per pupil, and adjusted tax rates in unified districts.

Revenues Per Pupil.   Reform has improved wealth neutrality with regard to general revenues. The elasticity of general revenue per pupil with respect to adjusted wealth per pupil declined about one-third after reform.

The elasticities of general revenue per pupil with respect to household income per pupil dropped even more sharply. They are about 60 percent lower in the postreform years.

Reform has substantially improved the degree to which general revenue per pupil in unified districts reflects local effort, as evidenced by the local property tax rate levied for education. In the 1970 to 1972 period, general revenue per pupil was negatively related to adjusted tax rates. The relationship turned positive with reform, but the magnitude of the elasticity consistently declined. The improvement in ex ante fiscal neutrality brought about by reform is apparently eroding over time.

Similar patterns prevail for the other four revenue measures in Table 4–10. In general, we find revenues per pupil highly dependent on wealth per pupil before reform. There is a roughly one-third de-

Wealth, Household Income, and Adjusted Tax Rates: California Unified Districts, 1970–76.

Dependent/Independent Variable	1970–71	1971–72	1972–73	1973–74	1974–75	1975–76	1976–77
General revenue							
Adjusted wealth	0.312	0.344	0.350	0.265	0.251	0.214	0.221
Household income	0.208	0.176	0.093	0.142	0.090	0.097	0.084
Adjusted tax rate	−0.141	−0.151	−0.318	0.287	0.204	0.069	0.062
General + PL 874 revenue							
Adjusted wealth	0.289	0.320	0.332	0.250	0.236	0.203	0.205
Household income	0.210	0.185	0.099	0.151	0.101	0.106	0.093
Adjusted tax rate	−0.186	−0.207	−0.351	0.216	0.152	0.039	0.037
Local + state revenue							
Adjusted wealth	0.309	0.346	0.347	0.271	0.256	0.221	0.219
Household income	0.223	0.174	0.113	0.133	0.089	0.092	0.080
Adjusted tax rate	−0.123	−0.145	−0.288	0.299	0.212	0.075	0.076
Local + state + PL 874 revenue							
Adjusted wealth	0.287	0.323	0.330	0.257	0.242	0.211	0.204
Household income	0.224	0.182	0.118	0.141	0.098	0.100	0.088
Adjusted tax rate	−0.165	−0.198	−0.319	0.233	0.164	0.048	0.052
Total revenue							
Adjusted wealth	0.298	0.321	0.333	0.260	0.251	0.207	0.195
Household income	0.192	0.150	0.092	0.114	0.072	0.076	0.065
Adjusted tax rate	−0.178	−0.178	−0.315	0.225	0.223	0.082	0.097
Instructional expenditures							
Adjusted wealth	0.224	0.235	0.256	0.249	0.248	0.217	0.179
Household income	0.183	0.204	0.182	0.131	0.135	0.118	0.110
Adjusted tax rate	−0.045	−0.056	−0.113	0.240	0.126	−0.007	−0.003
Adjusted tax rates							
Adjusted wealth	−0.206	−0.204	−0.239	0.036	−0.029	−0.097	−0.089
Household income	−0.012	−0.018	0.012	0.129	−0.008	0.012	−0.001

71

cline in elasticity in the postreform era; by all measures, however, revenues remain highly dependent on adjusted wealth per pupil.

Household income per pupil is positively related to each revenue measure in all years. The elasticity of revenues with respect to household income per pupil declined sharply between 1970 and 1972, jumped about 50 percent in the first year of reform, 1973, and then declined through 1976. By 1976, the elasticities were 35 to 45 percent of their 1970 values, but only a little below their 1972 values. It appears that, if anything, reform delayed an ongoing improvement in income neutrality.

Adjusted tax rates were negatively related to each revenue measure in each prereform year, and positively related to revenues after reform. And, in the reform years, the elasticity of revenues with respect to the adjusted tax rate has declined over time.

Instructional Expenditures Per Pupil.   Reform has somewhat improved the wealth neutrality of instructional expenditures per pupil. Reform has seen a much more dramatic decline in the relationship between instructional expenditures per pupil and household income per pupil, but household income per pupil has remained positively related to instructional expenditures per pupil.

Adjusted Tax Rates.   Reform has sharply reduced the degree to which adjusted tax rates vary with adjusted wealth per pupil. The elasticity of the adjusted tax rate with respect to the adjusted wealth per pupil is negative in every year except 1973, indicating that higher wealth districts enjoy lower local property taxes. The elasticities for 1975 and 1976, however, are lower than they were before reform. Household income per pupil was not a very important determinant of a district's local property tax prior to reform. Its elasticity is trivial in every year except 1973.

Winners and Losers

In the prereform years, revenues were becoming less equally distributed among different types of California's unified school districts. Reform generally brought about greater equality. (See Table 4–11.)

Revenues Per Pupil.   Average per-pupil revenues in the smaller districts were approximately equal to those in the larger districts in 1970, but the larger ones gained over the smaller in 1971 and gained yet more in 1972. By the latter year, average revenues in the smaller districts were only 91 percent of those in the larger. Reform brought that figure back up to about 99 percent.

A similar pattern is observed with respect to urbanization. In 1970, the less urban districts had per-pupil revenues 94 to 95 percent of those in the more urban, and lost further ground through 1971 and 1972. Reform restored that figure to about 95 percent.

In 1970, the more minority districts had a 3 to 5 percent revenue advantage over more white districts (10 percent in the case of total revenues). By 1972, their advantage rose to 13 to 20 percent, but, with reform, subsided to 3 to 12 percent.

There was a fairly strong trend in favor of districts serving poorer populations prior to reform; it was followed by substantial equalization in 1973.

Instructional Expenditures Per Pupil.   Before reform, instructional expenditures per pupil were somewhat greater in the larger, the more urban, the less white, and the more poverty-prone districts. Reform has tended to equalize matters.

Adjusted Tax Rates.   Prior to reform, tax rates were about the same in large and small unified districts. After reform, the smaller districts had a clear advantage, with adjusted taxes only 93 to 96 percent of those in larger districts. The less urban districts previously had 2 to 5 percent higher adjusted tax rates than those of the more urban districts, but somewhat lower ones after reform. Districts serving heavily white populations had tax rates slightly above (a percentage point or two) those levied by more minority districts, but the latter substantially raised their tax rates after reform, reaching levels 2 to 7 percent higher than the tax rates in the more white districts.

The one category in which reform seems to have had an equalizing effect on the distribution of tax rates is the percentage of a district's population in poverty. Whereas tax rates in the more poverty-prone districts previously had been 6 to 9 percent lower than those in better-off districts, in 1976 they were about 1 percent greater.

SUMMARY AND CONCLUSIONS

Roughly two-thirds of California's public school pupils attend schools in unified districts; reform has reduced disparities in the per-pupil dis-

Table 4–11. Distribution of Revenues, Instructional Expenditures, and Adjusted Tax Rates by District Characteristic: California Unified Districts, 1970–76.

District Characteristic	Ratio of Mean for Students below Median to Mean for Students above Median						
	1970–71	1971–72	1972–73	1973–74	1974–75	1975–76	1976–77
General revenue							
Size	1.00	0.97	0.91	0.99	0.97	0.98	0.99
% urban	0.94	0.91	0.87	0.95	0.93	0.94	0.96
% white	1.03	1.05	1.13	1.03	1.05	1.04	1.02
% poverty	0.99	0.97	0.93	1.00	0.97	0.98	0.98
General + PL 874 revenue							
Size	1.00	0.98	0.92	1.00	0.98	0.98	1.00
% urban	0.95	0.93	0.89	0.96	0.95	0.95	0.97
% white	1.05	1.06	1.14	1.04	1.06	1.05	1.04
% poverty	0.99	0.97	0.93	1.00	0.97	0.98	0.98
Local + state revenue							
Size	1.00	0.96	0.91	0.97	0.96	0.96	0.97
% urban	0.95	0.91	0.89	0.94	0.93	0.94	0.95
% white	1.04	1.07	1.13	1.06	1.08	1.07	1.06
% poverty	0.98	0.96	0.93	0.97	0.94	0.95	0.95

Local + state + PL 874 revenue							
Size	1.00	0.97	0.92	0.98	0.96	0.96	0.97
% urban	0.96	0.93	0.90	0.95	0.94	0.95	0.96
% white	1.05	1.08	1.14	1.07	1.09	1.08	1.07
% poverty	0.99	0.96	0.93	0.97	0.94	0.95	0.95
Total revenue							
Size	0.97	0.94	0.89	0.95	0.93	0.94	0.95
% urban	0.94	0.91	0.88	0.93	0.92	0.92	0.94
% white	1.10	1.13	1.20	1.12	1.14	1.13	1.11
% poverty	0.93	0.91	0.88	0.92	0.89	0.90	0.91
Instructional expenditures							
Size	0.96	0.97	0.95	0.94	0.98	1.01	0.99
% urban	0.96	0.98	0.96	0.95	0.98	1.01	1.03
% white	1.08	1.08	1.10	1.10	1.04	1.01	0.99
% poverty	0.96	0.97	0.95	0.94	0.98	1.00	1.03
Adjusted tax rates							
Size	1.00	0.98	1.00	0.97	0.93	0.96	0.96
% urban	1.04	1.02	1.05	1.00	0.93	0.98	0.97
% white	0.99	0.99	0.98	1.02	1.07	1.02	1.04
% poverty	1.07	1.07	1.09	1.04	0.97	1.01	0.99

tributions of revenues by 32 percent (in terms of the coefficient of variation) to 36 percent (in terms of the relative deviation from the median). Elementary districts enroll about 20 percent of the students; they have experienced some decline in revenue disparities, on the order of 20 percent. Reform has not done much to reduce disparities in the distributions of revenues among students in high school districts, but these districts enroll only about 10 percent of the state's students.

Reform has had far less impact on disparities in the distribution of instructional expenditures per pupil among districts of any type. However, these expenditures were more evenly distributed than revenues before reform. It appears that among districts of all types, those whose revenues were high before reform allocated a disproportionately large share of their revenues to noninstructional purposes. The reverse was true for districts with lower revenues per pupil; when reform substantially increased their budgets, they devoted most of their new revenues to "catching up" on instructional resources.

Reform has substantially reduced disparities in tax rates among districts of all three types.

Wealth neutrality has improved with reform, but revenues remain highly dependent on property tax bases in all three types of districts. Income neutrality has improved even more, but income continues to be a major determinant of elementary and secondary school districts' revenues. There has been only a slight increase in the degree to which high school and unified districts' tax rates are associated with their revenues, and little change in the association between elementary districts' tax rates and their revenues. All in all, school districts of all types now find their revenues somewhat more dependent on their fiscal efforts and less so on the size of their tax base and the income of their community. Despite these improvements, however, the wealthier districts (in the sense of both tax base and income) retained much of their revenue-raising advantages over the less wealthy districts.

Reform has not profoundly affected the distributions of revenues or instructional expenditures between large and small, more urban and less urban, or more white and less white districts. The more poverty-prone elementary and high school districts lost relative to their better-off counterparts. The kinds of districts that realized relatively high per-pupil revenues before reform generally continued to do so, and to roughly the same degree, after reform.

The distributions of tax rates have changed considerably, however. Larger elementary and high school districts decreased their tax rates relative to their smaller counterparts. But the larger unified districts increased theirs relative to smaller ones. The same pattern, by district type, holds for the less urban and the more urban districts. Tax rates in all three types of districts grew in the more minority districts relative to more white districts, but declined in better-off districts relative to the more poverty-prone.

California tried to equalize by raising the level of low-spending districts while capping high-spending districts. The first year of reform saw a dramatic increase in state aid (see Table 4–1) channeled to lower spending districts through a higher level foundation plan; and the distributions of revenues became more equal, particularly in the unified districts. But the revenue limits constrained the growth of revenues in both low-spending and high-spending districts: The caps that were intended to hold down revenue growth in high-spending districts, so that the low-spending districts could catch up, also limited the rate at which the latter could increase their revenues. The consequence was that increases in state aid had to be at least partially translated into tax relief.

If one takes the view that the quality of education is more closely related to instructional than to other expenditures, California's reform has accomplished little. Instructional expenditures per pupil became only slightly more equally distributed, and they are neither more nor less related to districts' wealth. It appears that low-revenue-per-pupil districts that had to get along with meager noninstructional resources before reform used most of their newly acquired funds to catch up in this area.

Finally, California's reform has significantly contributed to taxpayer equity. Before reform, low-spending districts levied notably higher local property tax rates than did high-spending districts. The combination of increased state aid and revenue limits enabled them to reduce their tax rates substantially.

5 THE EFFECTS OF REFORM IN FLORIDA

SCHOOL FINANCE IN FLORIDA

Florida supports its schools through a variable-level foundation plan. Prior to 1973, each district's foundation level was determined by the sum of allowances for salaries, transportation, and other current expense. From this total was subtracted the required local contribution: 90 percent of the calculated yield of a 6-mill local levy in 1972. The balance was provided by the state as its share of the cost of the program.

Foundation program salary allowances for instructional personnel were based on instructional unit salary values, which provided allotments ranging from $2,800 to $9,500, depending on the rank of the teaching certificate held and years of Florida teaching service. (The unit salary value for a beginning teacher with a bachelor's degree was $5,300 in 1972.) The transportation allowance depended on the density of a district and the number of one-way miles traveled the previous year. Allocations varied from $61.20 per mile to $43.20 per mile. In addition, $6,570 per instructional unit was allowed for other current expenses.

A small fund (less than 2 percent of the foundation program) was distributed to districts on a pro rata basis for each pupil in average daily attendance (ADA) in grades 1–12. In 1972, this distribution was about $10 per pupil.

79

A State Textbook Commission Fund was established for textbook purchases. It provided funds to districts according to their ADA and average book replacement costs.

A portion of the Florida Racing Commission Fund was distributed to school districts for teachers' salaries or pupil transportation unless otherwise allocated by the county commissioners. This fund was divided equally among counties.

Florida maintains several small programs for support of capital costs and driver education. These funds generally are distributed on the basis of ADA, although some are available only for demonstrated program need.

In 1973, when Florida reformed its system, the state retained the variable-level foundation approach, but revised the procedure used to calculate each district's foundation level. Weights, or relative ratios of support, were assigned to each of twenty-six programs: three basic programs corresponding to regular students in grades K–3, 4–9, and 10–12; eight programs for full-time special education students; seven programs for students who need special services for less than half their time in school; six programs for vocational technical students; and two programs for adult education students. Weights ranged from 1.0 for grades 4–9 to 15.0 for the homebound. The number of full-time-equivalent students in each program is multiplied by the program weight and then multiplied by the base student value, which is annually set by the legislature ($745 in 1975). The sum of the program entitlements, adjusted by the cost-of-living index for the county in which the district is located, is the district's foundation level. From this is subtracted the required local effort—the calculated yield from 6.2931 mills in 1975— applied to assessed valuation. The balance is provided by the state as its share of the cost of the program.

Supplemental allocations are computed for transportation, elementary counselors, and occupational specialists. Adjustments for vocational and exceptional programs are made to keep within the total level of state funding. (This was approximately 97 percent for 1974– 75.) Districts may generate additional funds over the minimum up to 8 mills. State Racing Commission funds are distributed to each county in equal amounts; counties may, at their own discretion, share this revenue with school districts.

Table 5–1 provides summary data on Florida school districts and their revenues by source for the 1972–73 and 1975–76 school years.

Table 5–1. Summary of Florida School Districts (dollar amounts in thousands).

	Year	
Item	1972–73	1975–76
Number of districts	67	67
Assessed valuation	59,894,288	81,274,735
Average daily attendance	1,466,001	1,567,481
Revenue		
Federal	137,180	243,696
State[a]	795,422	1,163,497
Local	509,026	864,227
Total, all sources	1,441,628	2,271,420

[a]Includes Racing Commission distributions of $14,000,000 in 1972, and $14,640,048 in 1975.

DATA AND DEFINITIONS

We obtained data on Florida for 1972–73 from files maintained by the National Conference on State Legislatures, and for 1975–76 from the *Annual Report of the Commissioner of Education.*

For 1972, the year before reform, we include in general per-pupil revenues all local revenues paid into either the general fund or the contracted program fund. The latter includes revenues from gifts, grants, and bequests, and from some other miscellaneous sources. General revenues per pupil also include the district's receipt from the foundation program, minus the allowance for transportation, plus its receipts of Racing Commission funds and its receipts from the state's ad valorem tax reduction fund.

Florida explicitly includes transportation allowance in computing each district's foundation level, but most other states treat transportation support as a categorical program. To facilitate comparisons between Florida and the other four states—all of which treat transportation support as a categorical program—we compute general revenues per pupil to Florida districts net of transportation.

State Racing Commission funds are, of course, general state aid to school districts and are so treated in our calculations.

All other current revenues from state sources are treated as state categorical revenues, including all state revenues paid into the contracted programs fund.

Our data did not specifically identify districts' receipts of impact aid. As a proxy for Public Law (PL) 874 receipts, we use federal direct aid paid into a school district's general fund. Federal direct payments are primarily impact aid, although receipts from miscellaneous small federal programs are included as well.

Total federal revenues include revenues from all federal programs, both those paid directly to a district and those distributed to districts through the state.

The adjusted local property tax rate is based on the nominal district school tax levy. Florida regularly conducts sales-assessment ratio studies and adjusts the foundation program's required contribution in order that districts do not receive state funds for underassessment. We use each district's factor to adjust its assessed value to market value, and its nominal tax rate to the tax rate effectively levied on market values.

Both finance and census data were available for all sixty-seven districts in both years.

THE EFFECT OF PUPIL WEIGHTS IN FLORIDA

We examined the distribution of weighted pupils among the state's districts. It was virtually identical to the distribution of (unweighted) pupils. The simple correlation between the two was 0.9999.[1] We computed the coefficient of variation, the relative deviation from the median, the quadratic regressions for each variable on wealth, income, and tax rates, and the distributions of each variable between districts below and above the median in size, percentage minority, percentage white, and percentage in poverty for both weighted and unweighted pupils. The results were identical to the level of precision shown in our text tables in every case. The results discussed below are for unweighted pupils. Except for means and medians, the corresponding results for weighted pupils are identical.

[1]Regressing weighted pupils (W) on pupils (P) yields the following results:

$$W = -173.6 + 1.265P; R^2 = 0.9997; F = 22392.$$
$$(-1.3)\quad(473.2)$$

THE DISTRIBUTION OF REVENUES, INSTRUCTIONAL EXPENDITURES, AND ADJUSTED TAX RATES

We examine the effects of Florida's reform on the distribution of revenues per pupil at six levels of aggregation: general revenues exclusive of Racing Commission funds, general revenues (inclusive of Racing Commission funds), general plus PL 874 revenues, local plus state revenues, local plus state plus PL 874 revenues, and total revenues (see Table 5–2). In computing the measures, we weighted by the number of pupils (FTE) in each district.

General revenues per pupil exclusive of Racing Commission funds grew about 42 percent between 1972 and 1975. The coefficient of variation increased by 1 percentage point, and the relative deviation from the median grew by 3 percentage points, an increase of about three-eighths.

Racing Commission funds provided about $10 per pupil, and PL 874 about $20, in both 1972 and 1975. Coefficients of variation and relative deviations from the median in each year are the same for general revenues per pupil, exclusive of Racing Commission funds, general revenues per pupil, and general plus PL 874 revenues per pupil. Revenues from the Racing Commission and from the impact aid program have no effect on the distribution of revenues among Florida's students.

Local plus state revenues per pupil, local plus state plus PL 874 revenues per pupil, and total revenues per pupil also grew about 40 percent between 1972 and 1975. At these levels of aggregation, we observe lower coefficients of variation and somewhat larger relative deviations from the median in 1972. It appears that before reform, state categorical distributions had a disequalizing effect. The coefficient of variation for local plus state revenues per pupil was 2 percentage points higher than for general revenues per pupil that year. Because the difference between the two measures is state categorical revenues, disproportionately high (low) state categorical revenues must have been distributed to districts that had relatively high (low) general revenues per pupil. Conversely, in 1975, state categorical revenue appears to have had an equalizing effect, in that both distributional measures are lower for local plus state revenues than for general revenue.

Florida's categorical programs provided somewhat less than $20 per pupil in 1972. Reform essentially consisted of adjusting districts' state

Table 5–2. Measures of the Distribution of Revenues, Instructional Expenditures, and Adjusted Tax Rates: Florida Districts, 1972 and 1975.

Measure	1972–73	1975–76
General revenue less Racing Commission funds		
Mean	785	1,119
Coefficient of variation	0.12	0.13
Median	765	1,089
Relative deviation	0.08	0.11
General revenue		
Mean	795	1,128
Coefficient of variation	0.12	0.13
Median	780	1,089
Relative deviation	0.08	0.10
General + PL 874 revenue		
Mean	815	1,149
Coefficient of variation	0.12	0.13
Median	790	1,095
Relative deviation	0.08	0.11
Local + state revenue		
Mean	812	1,182
Coefficient of variation	0.14	0.12
Median	805	1,166
Relative deviation	.08	0.09
Local + state + PL 874 revenue		
Mean	831	1,203
Coefficient of variation	0.15	0.13
Median	814	1,178
Relative deviation	0.09	0.11
Total revenue		
Mean	902	1,334
Coefficient of variation	0.14	0.12
Median	897	1,301
Relative deviation	0.08	0.09
Instructional expenditures		
Mean	625	853
Coefficient of variation	0.12	0.14
Median	614	814
Relative deviation	0.07	0.11
Adjusted tax rates		
Mean	8.1	6.5
Coefficient of variation	0.11	0.10
Median	8.1	6.2
Relative deviation	0.08	0.09

Note: All revenue measures and instructional expenditures are dollars per pupil. Adjusted tax rates are mills.

general aid receipts for the presence of relatively large numbers of expensive-to-educate children. In essence, the traditional purposes of categorical programs are served through the general aid program. Despite this, Florida distributed about $55 per pupil in state categorical revenue in 1975.

Total revenues per pupil differ from local plus state plus PL 874 revenues per pupil by federal categorical aid per pupil. Per-pupil revenues from these programs amounted to about $70 in 1972 and about $130 in 1975. Federal categorical revenue was distributed in a mildly equalizing manner in both years. Both the coefficient of variation and the relative deviation from the median are lower for total revenues per pupil than for local plus state plus PL 874 revenues per pupil.

Reform has had essentially the same effect upon instructional expenditures per pupil as it had on the distributions of revenues per pupil. Between 1972 and 1975, instructional expenditures per pupil grew about 36 percent. The coefficient of variation increased about 16 percent—from 0.12 to 0.14—and the relative deviation from the median increased substantially—from 0.07 to 0.11.

Reform has brought about a substantial decline in adjusted local property tax rates, from about 8.1 mills in 1972 to about 6.45 mills in 1975. Disparities in adjusted local tax rates have not changed much over that period. The coefficient of variation declined slightly and the relative deviation from the median increased slightly.

WEALTH, INCOME, AND TAX NEUTRALITY

We performed quadratic regressions of revenues per pupil at each level of aggregation, instructional expenditures per pupil, and adjusted tax rates on adjusted wealth per pupil, on household income per pupil, and on adjusted tax rates. Table 5–3 shows the elasticity, at the mean, implied by each regression.

Wealth was significantly related to per-pupil revenues at each level of aggregation before reform and continued to be so afterward. Significance levels exceed 0.00005 in every case in both 1972 and 1975. Elasticities are about 0.2 in each instance. A 1 percent increase in wealth was accompanied by an increase in per-pupil revenues of about 0.2 percent.

Wealth was also significantly related to instructional expenditures per pupil before and after reform. The corresponding elasticities are very small. The sign changes with reform: Previously, a 1 percent in-

Table 5–3. Elasticity of Revenues, Instructional Expenditures, and Adjusted Tax Rates with Respect to Adjusted Wealth, Household Income, and Adjusted Tax Rates: Florida Districts, 1972 and 1975.

Dependent/Independent Variable	1972–73	1975–76
General revenue less Racing Commission funds		
Adjusted wealth	0.221	0.240
Household income	0.111	0.317
Adjusted tax rate	0.440	0.118
General revenue		
Adjusted wealth	0.201	0.224
Household income	0.064	0.289
Adjusted tax rate	0.395	0.086
General + PL 874 revenue		
Adjusted wealth	0.199	0.214
Household income	0.087	0.306
Adjusted tax rate	0.581	0.145
Local + state revenue		
Adjusted wealth	0.206	0.206
Household income	0.082	0.261
Adjusted tax rate	0.412	0.073
Local + state + PL 874 revenue		
Adjusted wealth	0.204	0.197
Household income	0.104	0.277
Adjusted tax rate	0.594	0.129
Total revenue		
Adjusted wealth	0.170	0.169
Household income	0.063	0.231
Adjusted tax rate	0.598	0.139
Instructional expenditures		
Adjusted wealth	0.183	0.213
Household income	0.099	0.348
Adjusted tax rate	0.467	0.084
Adjusted tax rates		
Adjusted wealth	0.025	-0.038
Household income	0.078	-0.006

crease in wealth was associated with a 0.2 percent increase in instructional expenditures per pupil; after reform, it was associated with an 0.04 percent decrease.

Reform had no effect on the significance of the relationship between tax rates and wealth. That relationship is not significant by conventional standards either before or after reform. The elasticity of the tax rate with respect to wealth is positive in both 1972 and 1975, suggesting that higher wealth districts generally levied higher tax rates in both years—three times higher in 1975. In view of the low significance levels, however, we cannot refute the hypothesis that both elasticities equal zero, and we therefore can attach little importance to their magnitudes.

The results for household income per pupil are startling. Revenues and instructional expenditures per pupil were not significantly related to household income per pupil in 1972, but became highly related after reform at each level of aggregation. The elasticity of revenues with respect to household income ranged from 0.06 to 0.1 in 1972 and from 0.27 to well over 0.3 after reform. The elasticity of instructional expenditures with respect to household income more than tripled between 1972 and 1975, from about 0.09 to over 0.34.

In 1972, on the average, districts serving low-income and high-income communities obtained equal revenues and spent the same amounts on instruction. Reform dramatically upset that balance in favor of high-income communities.

Prior to reform, revenues per pupil and instructional expenditures per pupil were significantly associated with adjusted tax rate at the 10 percent level. Communities that exerted greater efforts in the form of a higher effective local tax rate had somewhat higher revenues or instructional expenditures per pupil. The elasticities are in the range of 0.4 to 0.6; a 1 percent increase in the local property tax rate was associated with about a 0.5 percent increase in per pupil revenues and instructional expenditures. Both revenues and instructional expenditures became less dependent on effective tax rates with reform. The significant levels of regressions of revenues and instructional expenditures on adjusted tax rates and adjusted tax rates squared all declined in 1975 from their 1972 levels, though many remained significant at the 10 percent level. The corresponding elasticities plummeted to about one-fourth of their prereform levels. Florida has therefore greatly weakened the relationship between a community's tax effort and its schools' revenues and instructional expenditures.

Finally, we note that adjusted tax rates were not significantly related to either adjusted wealth or household income before reform. Afterward they remained so with respect to adjusted wealth, but became significantly related to household income after reform. The magnitude of the latter relationship (an elasticity of -0.006) is so small as to be negligible, however.

WINNERS AND LOSERS

To identify winners and losers among Florida's districts, we ranked all students in terms of a characteristic of their district and computed the ratio of the mean value of each variable of interest for those below the median to the mean value for those above the median (see Table 5–4). The four district characteristics considered were size, urbanization, the white percentage of the population, and percentage of the population living in families with family income below the poverty level.

In 1972, smaller districts tended to have lower revenues and instructional expenditures. Reform accentuated this pattern. For example, general revenues per pupil in the smaller districts were 98 percent of those in the larger districts. In 1975 they were 89 percent. Similar patterns are evident for each of the other revenue variables and for instructional expenditures, with the figures for the smaller districts falling from about 96 percent to 90 percent.

The distribution of revenues exhibits a broadly similar pattern among districts characterized by the percentage of their population residing in urban areas. Before reform, both average revenues and expenditures in the less urban districts were about 96 percent of those in the more urban. In 1975, that figure had declined to about 90 percent for revenues, and had eroded all the way down to 85 percent for instructional expenditures. The more urban districts have gained a solid advantage.

Reform has had little effect on the distribution of revenues between districts serving more heavily white populations and those serving more minority populations. Both before and after reform, the ratio is about 1.06. The more minority districts had about 6 percent higher per-pupil revenues and instructional expenditures than the largely white districts.

Reform brought about a dramatic shift in funding away from more poverty-prone districts to better-off districts. In 1972, the better-off districts had an advantage of about 6 percent in per-pupil revenues; by

Table 5–4. Distribution of Revenues, Instructional Expenditures, and Adjusted Tax Rates by District Characteristic: Florida Districts, 1972 and 1975.

District Characteristic	Ratio of Mean for Students below Median to Mean for Students above Median	
	1972–73	*1975–76*
General revenue less Racing Commission funds		
Size	0.96	0.89
% urban	0.96	0.88
% white	1.05	1.04
% poverty	1.06	1.19
General revenue		
Size	0.98	0.90
% urban	0.98	0.89
% white	1.05	1.04
% poverty	1.04	1.17
General + PL 874 revenue		
Size	0.97	0.89
% urban	0.96	0.88
% white	1.06	1.05
% poverty	1.06	1.18
Local + state revenue		
Size	0.97	0.91
% urban	0.97	0.91
% white	1.04	1.04
% poverty	1.05	1.15
Local + state + PL 874 revenue		
Size	0.96	0.90
% urban	0.95	0.89
% white	1.04	1.05
% poverty	1.07	1.16
Total revenue		
Size	0.97	0.92
% urban	0.97	0.92
% white	1.05	1.06
% poverty	1.03	1.13
Instructional expenditures		
Size	0.96	0.89
% urban	0.96	0.85
% white	1.06	1.10
% poverty	1.06	1.18
Adjusted tax rates		
Size	0.93	0.96
% urban	0.95	0.99
% white	1.05	1.05
% poverty	0.97	0.99

1975, that advantage had increased to between 15 and 20 percent.

Reform led to a more even distribution of tax rates among various types of districts. In 1972, tax rates in larger districts were about 7 percent greater than those in smaller districts; in 1975, they were only about 4 percent greater. Similarly, the less urban districts enjoyed tax rates about 5 percent below those of the more urban districts in 1972; that advantage was virtually eliminated by 1975. The less white districts levied higher property tax rates in 1972, and that pattern was significantly affected by reform. Districts serving populations less prone to poverty enjoyed somewhat lower tax rates (about 3 percent) than did districts serving more poverty-prone populations in 1972. That differential was also virtually eliminated by 1975.

SUMMARY AND CONCLUSIONS

Florida's reform system is ostensibly designed to channel greater state aid per pupil to districts that have relatively high numbers of expensive-to-educate pupils, or to serve counties in which the cost of living is relatively high, or to do both. In fact, the distribution of different types of pupils among districts is such that the distribution of weighted pupils is virtually identical to the distribution of pupils as a whole. Except for the cost adjustment and the tax rate limits, Florida's system is, for all practical purposes, a foundation plan. The cost adjustment strongly favors the more urban districts, particularly Dade County, and thus favors Florida's larger, more urban, higher income, and less poverty-prone districts.

Florida's reform has widened the disparities in per-pupil revenues and instructional expenditures. Both the coefficients of variation and the relative deviations from the median for the revenue measures that exclude state and federal categorical aid increased between 1972 and 1975. Disparities in the revenue measures that include categorical aid decreased over that period, but those declines resulted from the distribution of categorical revenues.

Reform has led to a substantially less fiscally neutral finance system. The degree of association between per-pupil revenues and wealth, and between instructional expenditures and wealth, remained high between 1972 and 1975. More important, districts' per-pupil revenues and instructional expenditures before reform were largely independent of the incomes of the communities they served. After reform, the relationship between each revenue and expenditure variable and household income per pupil turned highly significant. Reform, in the case of Florida, involved a shift from an income-neutral finance system to one that is significantly biased with respect to income.

The source of this shift is almost certainly the cost adjustment factor. Whether or not school resources cost more in a county where the cost of living is relatively high is an open question; but cost-of-living indexes are likely to be higher in counties where household incomes are higher. And the indexes being the basis for Florida's approach to cost adjustment, those counties receive disproportionate amounts of state general aid.

Finally, Florida's reform has benefited the larger and the more urban districts somewhat more than it has the smaller and the less urban; and it has very substantially benefited the less poverty-prone districts.

In sum, revenue disparities have widened somewhat with reform. If the cost-adjustment indexes and student weights are accurate indicators of varying resource costs faced by different districts and the cost of serving pupils with different needs, the postreform disparities may be justified on equity grounds. They were obtained, however, at the cost of some decrease in wealth neutrality and the emergence of an income bias. If the cost-adjustment factors or student weights are not accurate, Florida has borne these costs in order to shift from one unequal distribution of revenues to another.

6 THE EFFECTS OF REFORM IN KANSAS

This chapter analyzes the consequences of reform in Kansas for the distributions of revenues, instructional expenditures, and tax rates; for fiscal neutrality; and for various kinds of districts. Kansas's post-reform system distinguishes among three types of districts: districts whose enrollments are below 400, between 400 and 1,299, and 1,300 or more. We perform separate analyses for each type.

SCHOOL FINANCE IN KANSAS

The Prereform System

Kansas implemented its school finance reform in the 1973–74 school year. Prior to reform, the state distributed general aid to the schools through a foundation plan, a supplemental aid program, and an ad valorem tax reduction fund. Districts also received general revenues from counties.

Local revenues for general operating funds were obtained from the local property tax, an intangibles tax, and miscellaneous other local sources, including tuition and gifts. Districts were free to set their tax rates, but could not increase their budgets more than 5 percent over their previous budget without approval of the Board of Tax Appeals or a district referendum. Districts held annual budget meetings at which the budget was adopted by the electors.

Property taxes were the primary source of revenue for the county school funds. Counties had to levy the equivalent of 10 mills on adjusted valuation. These proceeds were distributed to districts according to their share of the county's resident pupils or certified employees.

The Kansas prereform system employed a variable foundation level approach, in which a district's state guarantee was based on its enrollment and the number, training, and experience of its certified district employees. District ability to pay was based on a county-wide economic index prorated to the district according to its share of certified employees in the county.

Each district was guaranteed an amount equal to its staff's total college hours (up to 210 per teacher) divided by 30, plus total years of experience (up to 15 per teacher) divided by 5, times a unit cost factor times a pupil-teacher ratio factor. In 1972, the dollar value per unit of teacher quality was set at $760. The pupil-teacher ratio factor was 1 if the district pupil-teacher ratio did not fall below the state minimum based on enrollment and number of high schools; if the ratio was below the state minimum, the factor was the district pupil-teacher ratio divided by the specified minimum. A district's ability to pay per certified employee was the product of the county economic index (the mean of the county's share of state total assessed valuation and state total income) and the statewide proceeds of a 10-mill tax divided by the number of county certified employees. The state foundation plan entitlement was the difference between the guarantee and the sum of the districts' ability to pay and nondistrict revenues. In addition, the state paid 70 percent of actual per-pupil transportation costs or density-based costs up to $32 per pupil.[1]

The state supplemental aid program was passed in 1970. It provided for a distribution to school districts based on the number of students and number of certificated employees, adjusted by an index factor from a scale according to adjusted valuation per pupil. In 1972, supplemental aid equaled $71.70 per pupil and $1,240 per certified staff. Districts with less than $4,000 adjusted valuation per pupil received 50

[1]Both general and transportation aid was received by 303 districts under the foundation program. Moscow, Mullenville, and Rolla districts received only transportation aid; Fort Leavenworth, Hutchinson, and Topeka received only general aid; and Edson received neither general nor transportation aid.

percent of these amounts; districts with $18,000 or more valuation per pupil received only 20 percent of the pupil and teacher calculation.

Approximately 7 percent of the state funds were distributed as an ad valorem tax reduction, some of which was distributed to districts and some to counties. This was distribution from the sales tax to districts that kept their tax rates below a maximum approved levy, and was not more than the difference between the proceeds of the maximum and of the actual levy. The amount for each district was based on the previous year's tax rates and assessed valuation. In 1972–73, 287 Kansas districts received $6,160,656 from this program.

Kansas distributed funds for special education (educable retarded, other exceptional children, and homebound children), driver training, and vocational education. The state's payment in these programs was a varying share of the approved total expense.

Federal funds contributed approximately 30 percent of all monies available for Kansas school operating funds in 1972–73. In selected individual districts, federal impact aid was an important source of revenues. Federal impact aid [Public Law (PL) 874] is received by 105 of Kansas's districts. The Junction ($1,549,512), Derby ($947,875), Fort Leavenworth ($927,813), and Wichita ($630,525) districts received nearly one-half the total funds available in the state. In Fort Leavenworth PL 874 funds were approximately one-half the district budget; in the other districts listed above, they were closer to one-fourth or less.

The Postreform System

The 1973 Kansas school finance reform replaced the state foundation and supplemental aid programs with a guaranteed tax base (GTB) program. The county school foundation fund was reduced from the 10-mill to the equivalent of a 2-mill tax on the 1971 assessed valuation. All districts received an income tax rebate. State aid continued for special education, vocational education, driver training, and pupil transportation. School districts were limited in their annual budget increases to the lower of 15 percent of the previous year's budget, or 5 percent of the median budget per pupil for Kansas districts in the same enrollment category.

The legislature annually sets "norm" budgets for districts in various enrollment-size categories and "norm" local effort rates. In 1973, for example, the norm budget per pupil was $936 for districts with enrollments below 40 average daily membership (ADM), $936 minus $0.2311 for each student in excess of 400 for districts with enrollments between 400 and 1,299, and $728 for districts with enrollments of 1,300 or above. The norm effort rate was 1.5 percent. Each district establishes its budget, subject to the budget growth limit, and computes the ratio of its budget to the norm budget for its enrollment category. The product of that ratio and the norm effort rate is its local effort rate. Local effort is then the product of the local effort rate and the sum of adjusted valuation and taxable income, each averaged over the previous three years. State equalization aid equals the difference between the district's budget and the sum of its local effort, PL 874 receipts, intangibles tax receipts, and county foundation aid.

The reform requires counties to levy a tax on all county property that will yield the same dollar amount as a 2-mill tax would have yielded in 1971. These proceeds to the county school foundation program are distributed to school districts that lie wholly within a county on the basis of their share of certified employees, and to school districts lying in more than one county on the basis of their share of resident pupils. The intangibles tax rate is the same throughout the state and the funds are distributed (by shares of certified employees or pupils) to districts in the counties where raised.

The 1973 reform plan counts impact aid as a local resource. Although impact aid was a small part of the total funds available to districts ($7.5 million of $420 million), these funds continued to be significant for some districts, particularly Fort Leavenworth. The state had a special allocation to that district that helped to offset some of the effect of counting all the impact aid. It is left out of all other state distributions for equalization. In 1974–75, 89 districts in Kansas received impact aid.

The school finance reform bill provided for a 10 percent (since raised to 15 percent) income tax rebate to school districts. Kansas residents, under a separate law, are required to identify their school district on their state income tax returns. The state distributes 10 percent of the actual Kansas collections from residents to districts. In effect, the state serves as a collection agent for a state-mandated district income tax that is one-ninth of the state income tax.

The state continues to pay for special education based on a fixed amount per special education teacher. A vocational education fund provides for expenses in vocational education not covered by federal

Table 6–1. Summary of Kansas School Districts (dollar amounts in thousands).

Item	1972–73	1973–74	1974–75
Number of districts	311	310	309
Adjusted valuation	8,921,000	9,902,000	11,644,000
Average daily membership	471,275	457,268	446,886
General Fund revenue[a]			
Federal	12,476	10,236	10,014
State	113,336	157,558	188,908
County	65,830	33,732	16,673
Local	179,861	175,574	204,421
Total, all sources	371,503	377,100	420,016

[a]Sources of revenues paid into the other funds are not available for all districts.

assistance or required district taxes. The state finances approved driver training courses through a special fund.

Table 6–1 provides summary data on Kansas school districts and their general fund revenues by source.

DATA AND DEFINITIONS

We obtained data on Kansas school district revenues, expenditures, tax rates, and assessed valuations from a file maintained by the National Conference of State Legislatures. These data were supplemented by information from the *Annual Statistical Report* published by the Kansas State Department of Education. The available data covered three years, 1972–73 through 1974–75. Because of Fort Leavenworth District's special circumstances, we excluded it from our analysis. Data problems forced the exclusion of three other districts in 1972, of two other districts in 1973, and of one other district in 1974. Table 6–2 contains data on districts for which we had finance data and for which we had both finance and census data.

Kansas school districts maintain separate fund accounting for eleven categories of expenditures and receipts: General Fund, Social Security Fund, Capital Outlay Fund, Vocational Education Fund, Transportation Fund, Driver Training Fund, Food Service Fund, Special Assessment Fund, and Retirement Fund. On current account, separate property tax mill levies are permitted for the General Fund, Social Security Fund, Vocational Education Fund, Special Education

Table 6–2. Available Finance and Census Data on Kansas Districts and Students, by Enrollment Level, 1972–73 through 1974–75.

Enrollment Level	Finance Data Available		Finance and Census Data Available	
	Districts	Students[a]	Districts	Students[a]
Below 400				
1972–73	66	16,300	40	11,433
1973–74	71	18,242	45	13,162
1974–75	73	18,668	49	14,296
Between 400 and 1,299				
1972–73	175	124,695	173	123,763
1973–74	172	123,684	171	123,198
1974–75	169	119,554	167	118,659
1,300 or more				
1972–73	66	327,297	65	322,215
1973–74	64	316,568	63	311,317
1974–75	65	308,643	64	303,285
All districts				
1972–73	307	468,292	278	457,411
1973–74	307	458,494	279	447,677
1974–75	307	446,865	280	436,240

[a]September 15 enrollment.

Fund, and for Workman's Compensation. Kansas provides aid to the General, Vocational Education, Transportation, Special Education, Coop Special Education, Driver Training, and Food Service funds.

We define general revenue per pupil as the sum of local revenues over all current accounts, county foundation aid, and state general aid. The latter included payments from the state foundation program and supplemental state aid, in the prereform year, and state equalization aid and the proceeds from the income tax rebate in the postreform years.

Because the income tax rebate program is unique, we define an additional variable, general revenue per pupil exclusive of income tax rebate funds, and examine how reform affected it.

State aid includes state payments into all current accounts. Our data did not provide federal aid revenues other than impact aid. Accordingly, we do not examine the effects of reform on total revenues in Kansas.

Kansas assesses property at 30 percent of market value. The state computes an adjusted value for each district that reconciles departure from that rate. We use ten-thirds of a district's state-adjusted value as the wealth measure. We sum a district's local mill levies for all current accounts, multiply by the ratio of assessed value to state-adjusted value, and then multiply by three-tenths to obtain the effective tax rate on market value.

Because the reform plan provides varying fiscal opportunities to districts of different sizes, we separately examine the effects of reform on districts with enrollments below 400, between 400 and 1,299, and 1,300 or more.

DISTRICTS WITH ADM BELOW 400

The Distribution of Revenues,
Instructional Expenditures, and
Adjusted Tax Rates

We examine the effects of reform on the distributions of revenues per pupil at five levels of aggregation: general revenues exclusive of income rebate funds, general revenues inclusive of income rebate funds, general plus PL 874 revenues, local plus state revenues, and local plus state plus PL 874 revenues. We also examine the effects of reform on the distributions of instructional expenditures per pupil and adjusted tax rates. Table 6–3 presents the measures we used. In computing the measures, we weighted by the number of pupils (ADM) in each district.

General revenue per pupil exclusive of income tax rebate funds grew about 6 percent between 1972 and 1973 and about 14 percent between 1973 and 1974. The coefficient of variation declined from 0.24 to 0.21 in the first year of reform, but then rose to 0.23 in the second year. The relative deviation from the median exhibits a similar pattern: declining sharply in the first year of reform and then growing to nearly its preform level in the second year.

General revenues per pupil (inclusive of income tax rebate funds) grew about 6 percent between 1972 and 1973 and then increased

Table 6–3.   Measures of the Distribution of Revenues, Instructional Expenditures, and Adjusted Tax Rates: Kansas Districts with ADM below 400, 1972–74.

Measure	1972–73	1973–74	1974–75
General revenue less tax rebate			
Mean	1,190	1,261	1,443
Coefficient of variation	0.24	0.21	0.23
Median	1,157	1,223	1,385
Relative deviation	0.18	0.15	0.17
General revenue			
Mean	1,190	1,266	1,480
Coefficient of variation	0.24	0.21	0.22
Median	1,157	1,229	1,420
Relative deviation	0.18	0.15	0.17
General + PL 874 revenue			
Mean	1,200	1,274	1,488
Coefficient of variation	0.23	0.21	0.22
Median	1,170	1,233	1,420
Relative deviation	0.17	0.15	0.17
Local + state revenue			
Mean	1,267	1,367	1,596
Coefficient of variation	0.24	0.21	0.22
Median	1,225	1,317	1,540
Relative deviation	0.19	0.16	0.16
Local + state + PL 874 revenue			
Mean	1,277	1,375	1,603
Coefficient of variation	0.23	0.20	0.22
Median	1,240	1,335	1,543
Relative deviation	0.18	0.15	0.16
Instructional expenditures			
Mean	746	761	848
Coefficient of variation	0.21	0.21	0.20
Median	728	745	831
Relative deviation	0.16	0.15	0.15
Adjusted tax rates			
Mean	5.0	5.7	5.9
Coefficient of variation	0.28	0.20	0.19
Median	5.1	5.7	5.9
Relative deviation	0.21	0.15	0.15

Note: All revenue measures and instructional expenditures are dollars per pupil. Adjusted tax rates are mills.

nearly 17 percent in 1974. Comparing general revenues per pupil with general revenues per pupil exclusive of income tax rebate funds shows that, in Kansas's smaller districts, income tax rebates provided about $5 per pupil in 1973 and over $35 per pupil in 1974. The coefficient of variation and the relative deviation from the median for the distribution of general revenues per pupil are approximately the same in each year as the comparable figures for the distribution of general revenues per pupil exclusive of income tax rebate funds. Thus, the rebate does not seem to have had a substantial effect on the distribution of revenues per pupil in Kansas's smaller districts.

General plus PL 874 revenues per pupil tend to be about $8 to $10 greater than general revenue per pupil; impact aid therefore provides an average of about $8 per pupil to students in the smaller districts. The coefficient of variation and the relative deviation from the median for the distribution of general plus PL 874 revenues per pupil are in each year approximately equal to comparable figures for general revenues per pupil. PL 874 revenues appear to be distributed among smaller districts in approximately the same way as are general revenues, and thus have no effect on equalization.

The smaller districts received considerable revenues per pupil from state categorical programs: $77 per pupil in 1972, $100 in 1973, and $116 in 1974. The coefficients of variation for the distribution of local plus state revenues per pupil are approximately the same, year by year, as the coefficients of variation for general revenues per pupil. The relative deviation from the median is slightly higher in 1972 and somewhat lower in 1974, but the differences are not large. In the smaller districts, then, the distribution of state categorical revenues appears to be approximately the same as the distribution of general revenues per pupil.

Local plus state plus PL 874 revenues per pupil are distributed in about the same way as are revenues per pupil at lower levels of aggregation.

Instructional expenditures per pupil grew somewhat more slowly between 1972 and 1974 than did the revenue measures and appear to be more equally distributed among the smaller districts. The coefficient of variation is virtually constant over the three-year period, as is the relative deviation from the median. It appears that districts with higher revenues per pupil devoted a large share of those revenues to noninstructional purposes, and that lower revenue districts allocated most of their budgets to instruction, mainly teachers' salaries. In any event, reform has had only a slight effect, if any, on the distribution of instructional expenditures per pupil in the smaller districts.

The adjusted local property tax rate for education grew rapidly from 1972 to 1974, from slightly over 5 mills in the first year to just under 6 mills in the latter. Reform has, however, brought about very considerable equalization in the adjusted tax rates levied by the smaller districts. The coefficient of variation for this variable fell from 0.28 in 1972 to 0.20 in 1973, and to 0.19 in 1974. The relative deviation from the median exhibits a similar sharp drop between 1972 and 1974.

Wealth, Income, and Tax Neutrality

Table 6–4 shows the corresponding elasticities, computed at the mean, implied by quadratic regressions of revenues per pupil, at each level of aggregation, instructional expenditures per pupil, and adjusted tax rates on adjusted wealth per pupil, on household income per pupil, and on adjusted tax rates.

The results for the five revenue variables are virtually identical. Regressions of the revenue variables on adjusted wealth per pupil and adjusted wealth per pupil squared were highly significant in all three years. Elasticities of revenues with respect to wealth were about 0.48 in 1972. They generally fell to about 0.36 in 1973, and then grew to about 0.45 in 1974. Kansas's reform has not significantly affected ex post wealth neutrality in the distributions of revenues per pupil at any of the five levels of aggregation.

The five revenue variables also exhibit similar relationships to household income per pupil in each of the three years for which we have data. None of the variables are significantly related to household income per pupil in 1972 or in 1973, but all of them are in 1974.

Elasticities of revenues with respect to income generally increased with reform, from 0.1 to 0.2 in 1972 to 0.23 to 0.25 in 1974. Note that, before reform, the income elasticities tended to fall as the level of aggregation increased. This pattern is not observed after reform.

Quadratic regressions of each of the revenue variables on adjusted tax rates are insignificant in 1972, significant in 1973, and then insignificant again in 1974. There does not appear to be a substan-

Table 6–4. Elasticity of Revenues, Instructional Expenditures, and Adjusted Tax Rates with Respect to Adjusted Wealth, Household Income, and Adjusted Tax Rates: Kansas Districts with ADM below 400, 1972–74.

Dependent/Independent Variable	1972–73	1973–74	1974–75
General revenue less tax rebate			
Adjusted wealth	0.486	0.362	0.451
Household income	0.201	0.216	0.235
Adjusted tax rate	−0.094	0.554	0.132
General revenue			
Adjusted wealth	0.486	0.361	0.457
Household income	0.201	0.217	0.245
Adjusted tax rate	−0.094	0.553	0.122
General + PL 874 revenue			
Adjusted wealth	0.471	0.349	0.444
Household income	0.176	0.204	0.240
Adjusted tax rate	−0.097	0.549	0.145
Local + state revenue			
Adjusted wealth	0.493	0.373	0.448
Household income	0.125	0.173	0.240
Adjusted tax rate	−0.093	0.550	0.137
Local + state + PL 874 revenue			
Adjusted wealth	0.479	0.361	0.436
Household income	0.103	0.162	0.235
Adjusted tax rate	−0.096	0.546	0.158
Instructional expenditures			
Adjusted wealth	0.381	0.371	0.328
Household income	0.159	0.232	0.226
Adjusted tax rate	−0.125	0.491	0.093
Adjusted tax rates			
Adjusted wealth	−0.471	0.269	-0.124
Household income	−0.011	0.249	0.184

tial relationship between adjusted tax rates and any of the revenue variables.

Reform has had little effect on the wealth neutrality of instructional expenditures per pupil. There has been some increase in the degree to which instructional expenditures per pupil are associated with household income per pupil. The income regression in 1974 is significant.

The regressions on adjusted tax rates indicate a nonsignificant relationship in 1972, substantially increasing in significance in 1973 and 1974. However, the elasticity of per-pupil instructional expenditures with respect to the tax rate is negligible in 1974.

Wealthier districts had significantly lower tax rates before reform (elasticity = −0.471). The pattern was reversed in the first year of reform and then restored in the second reform year. Income was not significantly related to tax rates before reform or in the second year of reform.

Winners and Losers

We ranked all students in terms of the characteristics of their district and computed the ratio of the mean value of each revenue and expenditure variable for those below the median to the mean value of that variable for those above the median. The four characteristics considered were district size (ADM), the percentage of a district's population residing in urban areas, the percentage of a district's population who are white, and the percentage of a district's population living in families where the family income was below the poverty level. Table 6–5 presents the results.

The effect of reform on the distribution of revenues per pupil among pupils living in various types of districts is quite similar for each of the five revenue variables. In general, we find that in 1972 the smaller districts enjoyed revenues 31 to 34 percent greater than those in the larger. Reform reduced that advantage in the first year, 1973. In the second year, however, the ratio of the average value of each revenue variable for the students below the median in district size to the students above the median tended to return to its preform level. Overall, it appears that reform has had little or no effect on the distribution of revenues among students living in districts of varying sizes.

The less urban districts had average revenues 11 to 12 percent greater than those in the more urban districts in 1972. Reform has entirely eliminated this advantage; in fact, by 1974 it had turned into a slight disadvantage.

In 1972, the less white districts had average revenues per pupil that were only 84 or 85 percent of those for the white districts. Reform eliminated that disadvantage; in 1974, average revenues per pupil were approximately equal for both types of districts.

Table 6–5. Distribution of Revenues, Instructional Expenditures, and Adjusted Tax Rates by District Characteristic: Kansas Districts with ADM below 400, 1972–74.

District Characteristic	Ratio of Mean for Students below Median to Mean for Students above Median		
	1972–73	*1973–74*	*1974–75*
General revenue less tax rebate			
Size	1.34	1.23	1.30
% urban	1.12	1.10	0.98
% white	0.84	0.92	1.01
% poverty	0.98	1.00	1.20
General revenue			
Size	1.34	1.23	1.30
% urban	1.12	1.10	0.99
% white	0.84	0.92	0.98
% poverty	0.98	1.08	1.21
General + PL 874 revenue			
Size	1.32	1.23	1.30
% urban	1.10	1.09	0.99
% white	0.84	0.91	0.99
% poverty	0.97	1.08	1.20
Local + state revenue			
Size	1.33	1.22	1.30
% urban	1.13	1.11	0.99
% white	0.85	0.92	0.98
% poverty	0.97	1.08	1.20
Local + state + PL 874 revenue			
Size	1.31	1.22	1.30
% urban	1.11	1.10	0.99
% white	0.85	0.92	0.99
% poverty	0.96	1.07	1.19
Instructional expenditures			
Size	1.25	1.21	1.21
% urban			
% white	0.91	0.91	0.94
% poverty	1.05	1.09	1.11
Adjusted tax rates			
Size	0.95	1.17	0.99
% urban	1.00	1.04	0.95
% white	1.12	0.96	1.03
% poverty	0.90	1.05	1.08

Reform has substantially shifted the distribution of revenues toward the less poverty-prone districts. Before reform, in 1972, the better-off districts had 96 to 98 percent as much revenue per pupil as the more poverty-prone districts. That figure rose to about 120 percent in 1974.

The effects of reform on the distribution of instructional expenditures per pupil among the various district types are basically similar to its effects on revenues per pupil, though the changes are generally smaller in magnitude. Average instructional expenditures per pupil are substantially greater in the smaller districts than in the larger, although reform has somewhat narrowed the disparity. The prereform advantage of the less urban districts was substantially eliminated by reform, and the prereform advantage of heavily white districts was lessened though not fully eliminated in 1974. The more poverty-prone districts were at a disadvantage before reform, and still more so afterward.

Prior to reform the larger, the more white, and the less poverty-prone districts had average adjusted tax rates lower than those in the smaller, the less white, and the more poverty-prone districts. Reform substantially eliminated the advantages of the larger and the more white districts. In 1974, the rates were about the same in the larger and smaller districts, and were only slightly higher in the less white than in the more white districts. Reform turned the tables on the better-off districts: By 1974, their average adjusted tax rates were 8 percent higher than those in the more poverty-prone districts. Finally, tax rates were approximately equal in the less and more urban districts in 1972. The less urban gained from reform; in 1974, their rates were only 94 percent of those in the more urban districts.

DISTRICTS WITH ADM BETWEEN 400 AND 1,299

The Distribution of Revenues, Instructional Expenditures, and Adjusted Tax Rates

Table 6–6 presents data on medium-size Kansas districts.

General revenues per pupil grew about 13 percent between 1972 and 1973, and about 12 percent between 1973 and 1974. The coefficient of variation declined with the introduction of reform in 1973, but increased to nearly its prereform level in 1974. The relative deviation

Table 6–6. Measures of the Distribution of Revenues, Instructional Expenditures, and Adjusted Tax Rates: Kansas Districts with ADM between 400 and 1,299, 1972–74.

Measure	1972–73	1973–74	1974–75
General revenue less tax rebate			
Mean	876	987	1,085
Coefficient of variation	0.21	0.18	0.20
Median	873	983	1,067
Relative deviation	0.17	0.14	0.15
General revenue			
Mean	876	991	1,114
Coefficient of variation	0.21	0.18	0.20
Median	873	984	1,090
Relative deviation	0.17	0.14	0.15
General + PL 874 revenue			
Mean	881	996	1,119
Coefficient of variation	0.21	0.18	0.20
Median	875	984	1,101
Relative deviation	0.16	0.14	0.15
Local + state revenue			
Mean	920	1,054	1,195
Coefficient of variation	0.21	0.18	0.20
Median	923	1,055	1,160
Relative deviation	0.17	0.14	0.15
Local + state + PL 874 revenue			
Mean	925	1,060	1,200
Coefficient of variation	0.21	0.18	0.19
Median	923	1,055	1,163
Relative deviation	0.17	0.14	0.15
Instructional expenditures			
Mean	595	621	688
Coefficient of variation	0.19	0.17	0.19
Median	580	613	678
Relative deviation	0.15	0.13	0.12
Adjusted tax rates			
Mean	5.8	5.4	6.0
Coefficient of variation	0.28	0.23	0.18
Median	5.7	5.2	6.0
Relative deviation	0.22	0.18	0.14

Note: All revenue measures and instructional expenditures are dollars per pupil. Adjusted tax rates are mills.

from the median exhibits a similar pattern, declining sharply between 1972 and 1973, and then growing between 1973 and 1974. In all, reform seems to have slightly reduced disparities in general revenue per pupil, but whether 1975 and subsequent years will see further increases in disparities, continuing the trend from 1973 to 1974, remains an open question.

Comparing general revenues per pupil exclusive of income tax rebate funds to general revenues per pupil (inclusive of income tax refunds), we see that the income tax rebate provided medium-size Kansas districts about $4 per pupil in 1973 and just under $30 per pupil in 1974. The rebate funds seem to have been distributed in about the same way as was general revenue per pupil. The coefficient of variation and the relative deviation from the median for general revenue per pupil are identical to those observed for general revenue per pupil exclusive of income tax rebate funds.

In the districts, PL 874 revenues averaged about $5 per pupil each year from 1972 to 1974. The distribution of general plus PL 874 revenues per pupil is approximately the same as the distribution of general revenues per pupil both before and after reform. PL 874 revenues, then, have not affected the distribution of revenues per pupil.

Local plus state revenues per pupil equals the sum of general revenues per pupil and state categorical revenues per pupil. Thus the difference between the results shown for this variable and those shown for general revenues per pupil indicates the effects of state categorical programs. These programs grew substantially between 1972, when they provided an average of $44 per pupil, through 1974, when they provided an average of $81. Despite their size and impressive rate of growth, the distribution of state categorical funds had not affected the distribution of revenues. Year by year, the coefficient of variation and the relative deviation from the median for general revenues per pupil are equal to the comparable measures for local plus state revenues per pupil.

Prior to reform, instructional expenditures per pupil averaged $595. The figure grew by about $25 per pupil in the first year of reform and then increased by $67 in the second year. The disparities in instructional expenditures per pupil declined sharply in the first year of reform, but in the second year, 1974, the coefficient of variation rose to its 1972 level. The relative deviation from the median, however, continued to decline in 1974. The standard deviation is based on squared deviations from the mean, whereas the relative deviation from the median is based upon absolute deviations from the median. The coefficient of variation is thus more sensitive than is the relative deviation from the median to changes in the tails of the distribution. The fact that the coefficient of variation for instructional expenditures per pupil went up between 1973 and 1974, while the relative deviation from the median declined, suggests that the distribution has become more spiky or peaked, with the observations generally pulling in closer to the center and the tails extending farther from the center.

Adjusted tax rates declined sharply in the first year of reform, from 5.78 mills to 5.39 mills, but then increased over 10 percent to nearly 6 mills in 1974. Reform has very substantially decreased disparities in the rates; the coefficient of variation and the relative deviation from the median declined sharply between 1972 and 1973, and again between 1973 and 1974.

Wealth, Income, and Tax Neutrality

Table 6–7 shows the elasticities implied by regressions of the five per-pupil revenue measures, instructional expenditures per pupil, and the adjusted tax rates on adjusted wealth per pupil and adjusted wealth per pupil squared, on household income per pupil and household income per pupil squared, and on adjusted tax rates and adjusted tax rates squared.

Reform has slightly improved the ex post wealth neutrality of revenues per pupil in the sense that the elasticities of revenues with respect to wealth are somewhat lower in the postreform years compared with 1972. However, all the revenue variables are highly dependent on adjusted wealth per pupil in all three years.

Household income is significantly related to revenues per pupil both before and after reform. The elasticity of revenues with respect to income increased by about two-thirds with reform. Whereas a 1 percent increase in income was associated with an increase in revenues of about 0.23 percent before reform, that figure rose to 0.36–0.37 percent after reform.

Adjusted tax rates were significantly related to revenues per pupil both before and after reform. However, reform changed the sign of the relationship. The elasticity of revenues with respect to the tax rate was negative in 1972; districts that levied lower tax rates had generally obtained higher per pupil revenues. Note the elasticities of the tax rate

Table 6–7. Elasticity of Revenues, Instructional Expenditures, and Adjusted Tax Rates with Respect to Adjusted Wealth, Household Income, and Adjusted Tax Rates: Kansas Districts with ADM between 400 and 1,299, 1972–74.

Dependent/Independent Variable	1972–73	1973–74	1974–75
General revenue less tax rebate			
Adjusted wealth	0.437	0.340	0.354
Household income	0.232	0.281	0.369
Adjusted tax rate	-0.220	0.429	0.170
General revenue			
Adjusted wealth	0.437	0.339	0.363
Household income	0.232	0.281	0.383
Adjusted tax rate	-0.220	0.428	0.165
General + PL 874 revenue			
Adjusted wealth	0.420	0.326	0.352
Household income	0.227	0.275	0.375
Adjusted tax rate	-0.209	0.420	0.168
Local + state revenue			
Adjusted wealth	0.453	0.356	0.375
Household income	0.215	0.272	0.378
Adjusted tax rate	-0.237	0.412	0.154
Local + state + PL 874 revenue			
Adjusted wealth	0.437	0.343	0.365
Household income	0.211	0.266	0.371
Adjusted tax rate	-0.227	0.405	0.156
Instructional expenditures			
Adjusted wealth	0.352	0.326	0.285
Household income	0.273	0.331	0.326
Adjusted tax rate	-0.201	0.376	0.204
Adjusted tax rates			
Adjusted wealth	-0.543	0.122	-0.046
Household income	-0.227	0.346	0.266

with respect to wealth and income for 1972: Both were negative. Higher wealth (and higher income) districts were able to levy lower tax rates and still realize higher revenues in comparison with lower wealth (and lower income) districts. After reform, the higher wealth districts continued to obtain higher revenues than did lower wealth districts, but they had to raise their tax rates to do so. The elasticity of revenues with respect to the tax rate is positive in the postreform years.

In general, we found that reform has brought about some improvement in wealth neutrality. However, each revenue variable remains highly dependent upon adjusted wealth per pupil in the postreform years. There has been an increase in the degree to which each revenue measure is related to household income per pupil. And there has been a sharp increase in the dependence of each revenue measure on adjusted tax rates between 1972 and the postreform years.

Reform has not improved the wealth neutrality of instructional expenditures per pupil. The significance levels for regressions of instructional expenditures on wealth are high in all years, and the elasticities for the postreform years are only slightly lower than in 1972. Quadratic regression of instructional expenditures per pupil squared was significant in all years. The elasticity of instructional expenditures is about the same in all three years. Overall, reform seems not to have substantially affected the relationship between household income per pupil and instructional expenditures per pupil.

Adjusted tax rates were significantly related to instructional expenditures per pupil in both prereform and postreform years. As was the case for revenues, the elasticity changed sign between 1972 and the postreform years. Reform has shifted the relationship between instructional expenditures per pupil and adjusted property tax rates: Higher spending (for instruction) districts that enjoyed lower tax rates have had to raise them.

In all years, adjusted wealth per pupil was a significant predictor of adjusted tax rates. The elasticity of the adjusted tax rate with respect to adjusted wealth per pupil was about -0.54 in the prereform years; that is, wealthier districts enjoyed lower property taxes and an increase of 1 percent in wealth per pupil was associated, at the mean, with a decrease of about 0.5 percent in the adjusted tax rate. Reform has substantially reduced the elasticity of the adjusted tax rates with respect to wealth. Conversely, household income, which has not been significantly related to adjusted tax rates prior to reform (the significance level was less than 0.10), became a significant predictor of the adjusted tax rate in the postreform years. The elasticity of the adjusted tax rate with respect to household income per pupil was positive in both 1973 and 1974. These results suggest that school districts serving higher income populations were levying somewhat higher local property taxes for education.

Winners and Losers

Table 6–8 shows how reform affected the distribution of revenues per pupil, instructional expenditures per pupil, and adjusted tax rates among various types of medium-sized Kansas school districts.

Among these districts, the smaller, the less urban, and those serving less minority populations tended to have greater general revenues per pupil exclusive of income tax rebate funds than did their larger, more urban, and less white counterparts in 1972. Reform has not affected any of these patterns, though it has somewhat lessened the disparities between various types of districts. In the postreform years, the smaller and medium-sized districts tended to have general revenues exclusive of income tax rebate funds about 14 percent larger than did the larger districts, down from a 17 percent advantage in 1972. The less urban districts in 1972 averaged about 11 percent greater general revenue exclusive of income tax rebate funds than did the more urban districts; they maintained their advantage through the reform years at the somewhat lower level of about 7 percent greater. There has been virtually no change in the distribution of general revenue exclusive of income tax rebate funds between the more white and the more minority districts. Students in more poverty-prone districts seem to have fared no better and no worse in terms of this variable than have students in better-off districts, either before or after reform.

The results of the other revenue measures are similar and need not be separately discussed. In general, the smaller districts had about 17 percent greater revenues per pupil before the reform, and their advantage over the larger districts declined to about 14 percent with reform. The more urban districts had 11 or 12 percent less revenues per pupil in 1972; they caught up slightly with reform, achieving average revenues by each measure that were only about 7 percent below those enjoyed by the less urban districts. Reform has achieved greater equality in the distribution of revenues between the more white and the more minority districts on each revenue measure: In 1972, the more minority districts had revenues about 90 percent of those accruing to students in the more white districts; that figure grew to about 94 percent by 1974. Students in districts serving less or more poverty-prone populations tended to have about equal revenues per pupil both before and after reform.

Reform has had little or no effect on the distribution of instructional expenditures per pupil among various kinds of districts. In 1972, those

Table 6–8. Distribution of Revenues, Instructional Expenditures, and Adjusted Tax Rates by District Characteristic: Kansas Districts with ADM between 400 and 1,299, 1972–74.

	Ratio of Mean for Students below Median to Mean for Students above Median		
District Characteristic	1972–73	1973–74	1974–75
General revenue less tax rebate			
Size	1.17	1.13	1.14
% urban	1.11	1.06	1.07
% white	0.93	0.95	0.94
% poverty	1.00	1.04	1.02
General revenue			
Size	1.17	1.13	1.14
% urban	1.11	1.06	1.07
% white	0.90	0.90	0.94
% poverty	1.00	0.99	1.01
General + PL 874 revenue			
Size	1.16	1.13	1.12
% urban	1.11	1.04	1.11
% white	0.90	0.93	0.94
% poverty	1.00	0.99	1.01
Local + state revenue			
Size	1.17	1.14	1.15
% urban	1.12	1.11	1.08
% white	0.89	0.92	0.93
% poverty	0.99	0.98	1.00
Local + state + PL 874 revenue			
Size	1.17	1.14	1.14
% urban	1.12	1.07	1.07
% white	0.89	0.92	0.93
% poverty	1.00	1.04	1.00
Instructional expenditures			
Size	1.12	1.12	1.14
% urban	1.07	1.05	1.05
% white	0.92	0.93	0.92
% poverty	1.01	1.00	1.01
Adjusted tax rates			
Size	0.93	0.93	0.97
% urban	0.89	0.96	0.94
% white	1.11	1.03	1.07
% poverty	1.05	1.07	1.02

expenditures tended to be lower in the larger and the more urban districts than in the smaller and less urban, and the relationship remained essentially unchanged in 1974. Instructional expenditures per pupil in the less white districts were about 92 percent of those in the more white, a relationship unchanged with reform. Finally, the distribution remains unchanged in more and less poverty-prone districts.

Reform has substantially equalized the distribution of adjusted tax rates among students living in various types of districts. Before reform, the smaller districts enjoyed tax rates about 93 percent of those levied in larger districts. By 1974, that figure had risen to 97 percent. A similar pattern holds for the less urban districts, where relative taxes grew from 89 percent to 94 percent of the rates in more urban districts. Tax rates in less white districts were about 11 percent higher than those in more white districts in 1972, but only about 7 percent higher in 1974. The less poverty-prone districts levied tax rates about 5 percent higher than those in more poverty-prone districts before reform. Reform reduced the difference to 2 percent in 1974.

DISTRICTS WITH ADM 1,300 AND ABOVE

The Distribution of Revenues, Instructional Expenditures, and Adjusted Tax Rates

Table 6–9 presents the mean, coefficient of variation, median, and relative deviation of the median for distribution of revenues per pupil, at five levels of aggregation, instructional expenditures per pupil, and adjusted tax rates.

General revenue per pupil in Kansas's large districts grew from $752 in 1972 to $890 in 1973 and over $1,000 in 1974. Disparities diminished at the same time: The coefficient of variation declined from 0.14 in 1972 to 0.11 in 1974, and the relative deviation from the median declined from 0.11 to 0.09.

The effect of the income tax rebate can be observed in the difference between the measures for general revenues per pupil and the measures for general revenues per pupil exclusive of income tax rebate funds. The rebate provided about $5 per pupil to large districts in 1973

Table 6–9. Measures of the Distribution of Revenues, Instructional Expenditures, and Adjusted Tax Rates: Kansas Districts with ADM 1,300 and above, 1972–74.

Measure	1972–73	1973–74	1974–75
General revenue less tax rebate			
Mean	752	885	985
Coefficient of variation	0.14	0.13	0.11
Median	766	884	992
Relative deviation	0.11	0.11	0.08
General revenue			
Mean	752	890	1,016
Coefficient of variation	0.14	0.13	0.11
Median	766	889	1,025
Relative deviation	0.11	0.11	0.09
General + PL 874 revenue			
Mean	772	907	1,035
Coefficient of variation	0.12	0.11	0.10
Median	776	890	1,030
Relative deviation	0.09	0.10	0.08
Local + state revenue			
Mean	775	922	1,070
Coefficient of variation	0.14	0.13	0.11
Median	782	954	1,078
Relative deviation	0.11	0.10	0.09
Local + state + PL 874 revenue			
Mean	795	940	1,090
Coefficient of variation	0.12	0.11	0.10
Median	792	954	1,088
Relative deviation	0.09	0.09	0.08
Instructional expenditures			
Mean	563	575	643
Coefficient of variation	0.11	0.09	0.09
Median	554	577	693
Relative deviation	0.09	0.08	0.08
Adjusted tax rates			
Mean	8.1	7.4	7.7
Coefficient of variation	0.22	0.23	0.15
Median	8.4	7.5	7.6
Relative deviation	0.17	0.19	0.13

Note: All revenue measures and instructional expenditures are dollars per pupil. Adjusted tax rates are mills.

and just over $30 in 1974. These additional funds had virtually no effect on the distribution of general revenues among pupils in the large districts. The coefficient of variation in each year is unaffected by inclusion of the income tax rebate funds; and the relative deviation from the median is unaffected by the inclusion of income tax rebate funds in 1973 and is marginally lower when rebate funds are not included in the revenue measure in 1974.

Local plus state revenue per pupil equals the sum of general revenue per pupil and state categorical revenue per pupil. The difference between the results shown for these two variables indicates the effects of state categorical programs. These programs provided about $23 per pupil to large districts in 1972, about $32 in 1973, and just under $55 in 1974. They have had virtually no effect on the distribution of revenues among pupils in the large districts. The coefficient of variation for local plus state revenue per pupil is identical in each year to that for general revenue per pupil. The relative deviations from the median for the two measures are also virtually the same year by year.

Kansas's large districts received about $20 per pupil in PL 874 revenues each year between 1972 and 1974. Before reform, those revenues had an equalizing effect. The coefficient of variation for general plus PL 874 revenue was two points lower than that for general revenue per pupil; the relative deviation from the median for general plus PL 874 revenue per pupil also was two points lower than that for general revenue. These patterns persist into the reform years: In both 1973 and 1974, the coefficient of variation and the relative deviation from the median are lower when PL 874 revenue is included in the revenue measure than they are when such revenue is excluded.

By every measure, prior to reform, instructional expenditures per pupil were more equally distributed than revenues per pupil. Reform has reduced disparities in those expenditures measured by both the coefficient of variation and the relative deviation from the median. Apparently, both before and after reform, districts with larger revenues per pupil spent more for noninstructional purposes, while districts with smaller revenues devoted a larger share to instruction.

The first year of reform saw a dramatic decline in the adjusted tax rate levied by Kansas's large districts, from over 8 mills to 7.38 mills. In 1974, however, tax rates rose to 7.7 mills. Reform has also dramatically narrowed disparities among the large districts' adjusted tax rates. The coefficient of variation declined from 0.22 in 1972 to 0.15 in 1974, and the relative deviation from the median from 0.17 to 0.13.

Wealth, Income, and Tax Neutrality

Table 6–10 shows the elasticities, at the mean, for the relevant variables. Reform has reduced the wealth elasticity of revenues per pupil, but revenues remain significantly related to adjusted wealth per pupil. Reform did not affect the relationships between revenues per pupil and household income: The regressions of revenues on household income are significant in all years, and the implied elasticities are about the same in 1973 and 1974 as they were in 1972. Before reform, revenues per pupil were related to adjusted tax rates at low levels of significance. Reform substantially changed that pattern. By 1972 the adjusted tax rate became as important a predictor of revenues per pupil as was adjusted wealth per pupil. The corresponding elasticities are much larger in the postreform era.

Instructional expenditures per pupil exhibit a similar pattern. Regressions are significant in all years for wealth, income, and the tax rate. There has been little change in the wealth or income elasticities of instructional expenditures; but its elasticity with respect to the adjusted tax rates substantially increased with reform.

Before reform, adjusted wealth per pupil was a significant predictor of adjusted tax rates. The elasticity of the adjusted tax rate with respect to adjusted per-pupil wealth was about -0.3 in the prereform year, meaning that wealthier districts enjoyed lower property tax rates and that a 1 percent increase in wealth per pupil was associated, at the mean, with a decrease of about 0.3 percent in the adjusted tax rate. Reform, however, has brought about a substantially lower wealth elasticity. The relationship between the adjusted tax rate and income is essentially unchanged.

Winners and Losers

Table 6–11 shows the effects of reform on the distribution of revenues per pupil, instructional expenditures per pupil, and adjusted tax rates among the students living in various types of large Kansas school districts.

Reform has had little effect on the distribution of general revenues. The ratio of general revenues per pupil for districts below the median in size, percentage of the population residing in urban areas, percen-

Table 6–10. Elasticity of Revenues, Instructional Expenditures, and Adjusted Tax Rates with Respect to Adjusted Wealth, Household Income, and Adjusted Tax Rates: Kansas Districts with ADM 1,300 and above, 1972–74.

Dependent/Independent Variable	1972–73	1973–74	1974–75
General revenue less tax rebate			
Adjusted wealth	0.381	0.204	0.215
Household income	0.254	0.270	0.234
Adjusted tax rate	0.180	0.352	0.410
General revenue			
Adjusted wealth	0.381	0.204	0.225
Household income	0.254	0.270	0.251
Adjusted tax rate	0.180	0.353	0.427
General + PL 874 revenue			
Adjusted wealth	0.219	0.111	0.141
Household income	0.201	0.240	0.213
Adjusted tax rate	0.141	0.322	0.353
Local + state revenue			
Adjusted wealth	0.379	0.221	0.246
Household income	0.235	0.229	0.234
Adjusted tax rate	0.182	0.310	0.376
Local + state + PL 874 revenue			
Adjusted wealth	0.221	0.131	0.166
Household income	0.184	0.200	0.198
Adjusted tax rate	0.144	0.280	0.306
Instructional expenditures			
Adjusted wealth	0.127	0.145	0.145
Household income	0.291	0.264	0.233
Adjusted tax rate	0.223	0.242	0.317
Adjusted tax rates			
Adjusted wealth	-0.277	-0.089	-0.086
Household income	0.411	0.644	0.442

tage of the population who are white, and percentage living in poverty, to the general revenues received by students in districts above the median, are virtually unchanged between 1972 and 1974.

Reform has affected the distribution of instructional expenditures per pupil. In 1974, expenditures in smaller districts were about 94 percent of those in the larger—up from 90 percent in 1972. Similarly, expenditures in the less urban districts in 1974 were about 94 percent of those in more urban districts—up from 89 percent in 1972. In 1972, more white districts spent slightly less per pupil than did the more minority districts; in 1974, they spent about 3 percent more. The less poverty-prone districts spent about 9 percent more than did the more poverty-prone.

Before reform, the smaller and the less urban of Kansas's large districts had substantially lower adjusted tax rates than their larger and more urban counterparts. Reform has slightly narrowed those disparities. The big winners, in Kansas, were the more white and better-off districts. Their adjusted tax rates had been much higher before reform, and remain higher after reform, but the differences between them and the less white and the more poverty-prone districts have been substantially reduced.

SUMMARY AND CONCLUSIONS

Kansas's reform plan has the basic structure of a guaranteed tax base system. In principle, each district determines its budget per pupil, recognizing that higher budgets require higher local effort. Within an enrollment category, low-wealth and high-wealth districts may opt for the same budget per pupil by exerting the same local effort. State equalization aid to the lower wealth district would be greater by an amount sufficient to compensate for the lesser local revenues it obtains in applying the effort rate to its lower wealth base.

However, Kansas appended budget-growth limits to the basic plan that fundamentally changed its character. Although lower spending districts are permitted larger budget increases than are the higher spending, the limits constrain the extent to which they can take advantage of power equalization. A district whose budget was low before reform is simply not allowed to select as high a budget as may be (and almost certainly is) selected by a district whose budget was higher before reform. The finance plan does little to close the budget disparities that existed before reform; instead, it uses state general aid to provide tax relief to the lower wealth districts.

In addition, the income tax rebate to a county is a flat percentage of the state income tax receipts from the county's residents. Consequently, rebates are larger where incomes are higher. Because these

Table 6–11. Distribution of Revenues, Instructional Expenditures, and Adjusted Tax Rates by District Characteristic: Kansas Districts with ADM 1,300 and above, 1972–74.

	Ratio of Mean for Students below Median to Mean for Students above Median		
District Characteristic	1972–73	1973–74	1974–75
General revenue less tax rebate			
Size	0.93	0.89	0.92
% urban	0.93	0.88	0.92
% white	0.96	1.01	0.97
% poverty	1.06	1.09	1.07
General revenue			
Size	0.93	0.89	0.92
% urban	0.93	0.88	0.92
% white	0.95	1.01	0.98
% poverty	1.06	1.09	1.07
General + PL 874 revenue			
Size	0.96	0.91	0.93
% urban	0.95	0.90	0.94
% white	0.98	1.03	0.99
% poverty	1.06	1.08	1.07
Local + state revenue			
Size	0.94	0.91	0.93
% urban	0.93	0.90	0.93
% white	0.96	1.00	0.97
% poverty	1.06	1.09	1.07
Local + state + PL 874 revenue			
Size	0.97	0.92	0.94
% urban	0.96	0.92	0.95
% white	0.98	1.02	0.98
% poverty	1.05	1.08	1.06
Instructional expenditures			
Size	0.90	0.93	0.94
% urban	0.89	0.93	0.94
% white	1.01	0.98	0.97
% poverty	1.09	1.07	1.06
Adjusted tax rates			
Size	0.78	0.73	0.80
% urban	0.75	0.72	0.80
% white	1.16	1.18	1.11
% poverty	1.24	1.20	1.12

funds cannot be used to increase school spending, they must supplant local property tax revenue within the approved budget. In this way, the income tax rebate provides tax relief to all districts, but particularly to higher income districts.

Kansas's reform does not appear to be addressed to the equalization issues that have motivated reform elsewhere. It might be described as a way to shift the school support burden from the property tax to the income and sales taxes. In fact, improving fiscal neutrality may not have been an important reform objective. The GTB nature of the basic plan is clearly oriented toward a fiscal neutrality standard, but the income tax rebate program as clearly violates that standard.

Our empirical results are pretty much what one might expect. Revenues per pupil were somewhat more equally distributed in 1974 than they were in 1972, particularly in the large districts. Coefficients of variation for the distribution of revenue at various levels of aggregation declined 5 to 10 percent among the small and medium districts and 15 to 20 percent among the large districts. The distribution of instructional expenditures per pupil among small and among medium districts is virtually unchanged with reform; the coefficient of variation among the large districts declined about 18 percent between 1972 and 1974. The distributions of adjusted tax rates, on the other hand, became much more equal for all three types of districts. The coefficient of variation fell by roughly one-third in each case.

Kansas's reform has had little effect on fiscal neutrality in any of the senses considered here. Association between per-pupil revenues or instructional expenditures and the adjusted property tax base are about the same after reform as they were before. Revenues and instructional expenditures per pupil are more closely related to household income per pupil in 1974 than they were in 1972 but, in both years, household income is a much weaker predictor of either revenues or instructional expenditures than is the adjusted property tax base. The adjusted tax rate was unrelated to revenues or expenditures in either year among the small districts. It was slightly related to revenues and instructional expenditures in both years for the medium districts and in the post-reform year for the large districts.

Reform's big winners among the small districts were the more urban, the less white, and the less poverty-prone. The distributions of revenues and instructional expenditures between different kinds of medium and large districts were not much affected by reform.

7 THE EFFECTS OF REFORM IN MICHIGAN

SCHOOL FINANCE IN MICHIGAN

Prior to reform, Michigan distributed general aid to the schools through a multilevel foundation program in which different foundation guarantees and computational tax rates applied to districts whose assessed value fell into different intervals. As many as four different intervals were used in the late 1960s, but two-stage systems were typical.

In 1972, the state foundation program was set at $715 or $644 per pupil, based on the assessed valuation per pupil in the district, with additional allowances for transportation, special education, and tuition. These funds are for general expenses of education, but a portion may be used for capital outlay and debt service. Additional categorical programs distribute a small share of the state support.

For school districts with less than $17,750 equalized assessed valuation per pupil in membership, the foundation program provided the difference between $715 per average daily membership (ADM) and the yield of a 20-mill tax on the state equalized assessed valuation. (At $17,749, this aid would be $360.02 per ADM.) For school districts with $17,750 equalized assessed valuation per ADM or more, the state guarantees the difference between $644 per ADM and the yield of a 16-mill tax. (At $17,750 assessed value per ADM, state aid would be $360 per ADM.)

To participate fully in the foundation program, districts were required to have a 9-mill tax rate; pro rata participation was permitted for districts with lower tax rates. A total of 579 Michigan districts participated in the foundation program.

The rest of the state funds were distributed on the basis of the costs of approved programs. The local share was defined as that part of the costs not paid by the state support.

The Michigan constitution provides for a maximum tax rate of 50 mills for current expenditure purposes. Counties can use an allocation board to allocate a maximum of 15 mills among taxing units, or the electorate may vote an allocation of 18 mills to the taxing jurisdictions. In either case, any proposed property tax above the 15-mill or 18-mill limit must be voted on by the electorate. Debt service and capital outlay taxes are separate from those current expenses. Also outside the 15-mill or 8-mill local limit, voters may organize intermediate districts for mentally or physically handicapped education. The local taxes for schools provided approximately one-half the total funds in 1972.

The reform plan provided each district with a fixed revenue per mill of tax rate for operating purposes. In 1973, districts were guaranteed $38 per mill per pupil on the first 22 mills of operating taxes. This amount is made up of the local revenue from the property tax and state aid, with state aid providing the difference between $38 per mill per pupil and the amount of local revenue. The amount of guarantee and the mill-levy guarantee were annually changed by the legislature to reflect the desired level of state support. In 1974, the guarantee was $39 per pupil per mill for the first 25 mills; in 1975, it was $42.40 per pupil per mill for the first 20 mills, and $38.25 per pupil per mill for the next 7 mills.

A phase-in period was provided to permit districts to make gradual adjustments from the foundation program. To protect districts against total dollar loss, several optional computations of state aid were possible during the first two years of the plan.

As an example of how the plan would work, a district with a state assessed valuation of $24,000 in 1973 and a tax rate of 24 mills would have raised $576 per pupil locally. The state share would be $308 per pupil; at 22 mills, the state guarantee is $836 per pupil and 22 mills of local revenue would raise only $528 per pupil. Since the district is taxing above 22 mills, it retains the $48 per pupil realized from the two additional mills of taxation and has available $884 per pupil to spend.

A small amount of basic membership aid continues to aid intermediate districts. This aid is distributed on a per-pupil basis, less the equivalent of a 0.2-mill tax on property.

Municipal overburden aid primarily assisted the Detroit school district. It is designed to reduce the level of local taxation required for schools in districts where non-school-operating local taxation exceeds the state average by more than 25 percent.

For debt service equalization, the state guarantees an equal mill rate per bonded debt per pupil. The total mills equalized in any district for both operating funds and debt service was limited to 22 mills (for 1973). The state reimbursement was the amount necessary to lower the millage rate such that the yield from the millage rate and the state funds would satisfy the debt service requirements. The actual limit for debt service equalization was not increased in later years.

Special education and vocational education programs were included by the state's funding 75 percent of any additional costs they incurred above the costs of regular education for members in these programs.

Michigan continued to pay 75 percent of approved transportation costs to districts. Selected pupil-targeted programs were also funded by the state, either at a share of the cost or a specific amount per program professional. Some of the examples of pupil-targeted programs funded in this manner include reading support, alternative programs for pregnant students, alternative juvenile programs, and compensatory education.

Table 7–1 provides summary information on Michigan's school districts and their revenues by source.

DATA AND DEFINITIONS

Our data, obtained from the Michigan State Department of Education, span five years: 1971–72 through 1975–76. Limitations on the available data forced us to exclude all elementary districts and between one and seven K–12 districts in each year. Because our data did not include information on instructional expenditures per pupil, that variable is entirely omitted from the analyses. Table 7–2 shows the numbers of districts and students for which data were available in each year.

In all years, general revenue includes all revenue derived from local and intermediate sources and receipts from the state foundation program; all other revenues from state sources are treated as state

Table 7–1. Summary of Michigan School Districts (dollar amounts in thousands).

Item	1971–72	1972–73	1973–74	1974–75	1975–76
Number of districts	608	602	597	590	587
Assessed valuation	41,663,602	44,493,655	47,804,116	51,747,786	56,794,495
Average daily membership	2,206,408	2,187,818	2,155,669	2,135,867	2,127,917
General Fund Revenue					
Federal[a]	102,418	112,945	116,181	145,712	161,897
State	798,504	859,463	945,116	991,396	1,028,155
Intermediate	2,894	3,403	3,875	4,583	3,431
Local[b]	1,150,701	1,214,530	1,379,830	1,545,809	1,716,947
Total, all sources	2,054,517	2,190,341	2,445,002	2,687,500	2,910,430

[a]Includes state redistribution of federal funds.
[b]Includes gifts and bequests.

Table 7–2. Available Finance and Census Data on Michigan
K–12 Districts and Students, 1971–72 through 1975–76.

Year	Finance Data Available[a]		Finance and Census Data Available	
	Districts	Students	Districts	Students
1971–72	524	2,179,299	452	1,995,613
1972–73	523	2,157,223	451	1,975,135
1973–74	523	2,121,090	451	1,943,422
1974–75	523	2,100,243	451	1,925,087
1975–76	529	2,096,623	456	1,922,586

[a]Data were missing for five districts (27,109 students) in 1971, seven districts (30,595 students) in 1972, seven districts (34,579 students) in 1973, seven districts (35,624 students) in 1974, and one district (2,016 students) in 1975.

categorical revenues. Our data did not specifically identify receipts from the Public Law (PL) 874 program; instead, we used federal direct revenues which include impact aid, Head Start, emergency school assistance program funds, community action program funds, and other (negligible) federal programs. The bulk of direct federal revenues, however, are impact aid funds. Total federal revenues include federal direct revenues and all federal funds redistributed through the state.

Property is assessed at 50 percent of its fair market value; the state conducts assessment reviews to equalize assessed values. We divide the general fund tax rate by two to obtain the effective rate on market value, and double assessed values to obtain market value.

THE DISTRIBUTION OF REVENUES
AND ADJUSTED TAX RATES

Table 7–3 shows the mean, coefficient of variation, median, and relative deviation from the median for the distribution of revenue, at each level of aggregation, and adjusted tax rates.

It is apparent that reform brought substantial increases in general revenue per pupil: $115 in the first year of reform, $104 in the second, and $115 in the third. The coefficient of variation is virtually constant over the four-year period, and the relative deviation from the median is only a point or two lower in the postreform years.

The impact aid program provided about $15 per pupil in the first

Table 7–3. Measures of the Distribution of Revenues, Instructional Expenditures, and Adjusted Tax Rates: Michigan Districts, 1971–75.

Measure	1971 –72	1972 –73	1973 –74	1974 –75	1975 –76
General revenue					
Mean	830	884	999	1,103	1,218
Coefficient of variation	0.15	0.17	0.15	0.15	0.16
Median	790	861	962	1,076	1,186
Relative deviation	0.12	0.13	0.11	0.11	0.10
General + PL 874 revenue					
Mean	845	901	1,014	1,123	1,242
Coefficient of variation	0.15	0.17	0.15	0.14	0.16
Median	803	879	968	1,089	1,192
Relative deviation	0.11	0.13	0.11	0.11	0.11
Local + state revenue					
Mean	882	948	1,079	1,189	1,301
Coefficient of variation	0.15	0.15	0.14	0.13	0.16
Median	863	913	1,079	1,187	1,270
Relative deviation	0.11	0.12	0.10	0.10	0.10
Local + state + PL 874 revenue					
Mean	898	965	1,095	1,209	1,326
Coefficient of variation	0.15	0.15	0.14	0.14	0.17
Median	891	933	1,094	1,208	1,312
Relative deviation	0.11	0.12	0.10	0.10	0.10
Total revenue					
Mean	929	1,000	1,134	1,258	1,378
Coefficient of variation	0.15	0.15	0.14	0.14	0.17
Median	911	954	1,121	1,246	1,344
Relative deviation	0.12	0.11	0.11	0.11	0.11
Adjusted tax rates					
Mean	12.3	12.1	12.7	13.2	13.6
Coefficient of variation	0.20	0.24	0.18	0.15	0.14
Median	12.3	12.3	12.3	12.5	13.3
Relative deviation	0.17	0.20	0.15	0.13	0.11

Note: All revenue measures and instructional expenditures are dollars per pupil. Adjusted tax rates are mills.

three years, $20 in 1974, and $24 in 1975. These funds have had no effect on revenue disparities either before or after reform.

State categorical aid per pupil grew from about $52 in 1971 to about $83 in 1975. These revenues appear to have had a slightly equalizing effect in the first two years of reform, but that effect disappeared by 1975. The coefficient of variation and the relative deviation from the

128

median for the distributions of per-pupil local plus state revenue are generally about the same as the corresponding statistics for the distributions of general revenue per pupil.

Federal categorical revenues, amounting to $31 per pupil in 1971, grew to $52 per pupil in 1975. They do not seem to have affected disparities in per-pupil revenues. The coefficient of variation and relative deviaion from the median for total revenue per pupil are about the same each year as the comparable figures for local plus state plus PL 874 revenue per pupil.

Comparing the measures for general plus PL 874 revenue per pupil with those for total revenue per pupil, state and federal categorical aid amounted to about $84 in 1971 and grew to about $136 in 1975. These funds have not had a decided effect on the distribution of revenues. Year to year, the coefficients of variation and relative deviations from the median for the two variables are pretty much the same.

Adjusted tax rates have increased with reform, but disparities among them have narrowed considerably. By 1975, both the coefficient of variation and the relative deviation from the median had fallen to about two-thirds of their 1972 levels.

WEALTH, INCOME, AND TAX NEUTRALITY

Table 7–4 shows the elasticity of revenues per pupil, at each level of aggregation, and adjusted tax rates with respect to adjusted wealth per pupil, household income per pupil, and the adjusted tax rate.

The elasticities of the revenue variables with respect to wealth declined between 1971 and 1972, prior to reform. At lower levels of aggregation—for general revenues and general reform plus PL 874 revenues—the elasticity increased slightly with reform. When categorical revenues are included—for local plus state revenues, local plus state plus PL 874 revenues, and total revenue—the elasticity continued to decline through 1974, then increased by about 10 percent in 1975. All in all, reform seems to have had little effect on the relationship between revenues and wealth.

It may be that the 1971 results are atypical for some reason, and that the 1972 elasticities are characteristic of the wealth neutrality of Michigan's prereform plan. If so, reform has done nothing to improve wealth neutrality in Michigan. The postreform distributions of revenues excluding categorical aid are no more wealth-neutral than they

Table 7–4. Elasticity of Revenues, Instructional Expenditures, and Adjusted Tax Rates with Respect to Adjusted Wealth, Household Income, and Adjusted Tax Rates: Michigan Districts, 1971–75.

Dependent/Independent Variable	1971 –72	1972 –73	1973 –74	1974 –75	1975 –76
General revenue					
Adjusted wealth	0.251	.233	.240	.238	.249
Household income	0.271	.239	.238	.221	.201
Adjusted tax rate	0.504	.543	.610	.654	.689
General + PL 874 revenue					
Adjusted wealth	0.253	.235	.236	.233	.238
Household income	0.274	.252	.251	.233	.150
Adjusted tax rate	0.451	.498	.574	.636	.667
Local + state revenue					
Adjusted wealth	0.268	.240	.225	.215	.241
Household income	0.272	.247	.244	.233	.106
Adjusted tax rate	0.431	.457	.535	.581	.668
Local + state + PL 874 revenue					
Adjusted wealth	0.270	.241	.222	.211	.231
Household income	0.275	.259	.256	.244	.061
Adjusted tax rate	0.383	.416	.502	.565	.648
Total revenue					
Adjusted wealth	0.277	.248	.224	.202	.212
Household income	0.278	.269	.276	.270	− .013
Adjusted tax rate	0.343	.371	.482	.560	.622
Adjusted tax rates					
Adjusted wealth	0.111	.122	.131	.096	.081
Household income	0.266	.277	.270	.247	.251

were in 1972; and the slight improvements in wealth neutrality observed for the more aggregate revenue measures are attributable to the allocation of categorical aid. Conversely, 1972 may have been an atypical year. Compared with 1971, the postreform revenue elasticities do suggest improvement. But, again, the improvement is most noticeable for the revenue variables that include categorical assistance.

The elasticities of revenues with respect to income exhibit similar patterns in the first four years. The elasticity declined between 1971 and 1972 and then remained roughly constant through 1974. In 1975, the elasticities with respect to income dropped sharply at higher levels of aggregation. The distributions of local plus state plus PL 874 revenues and of total revenues were essentially income neutral in 1975.

Adjusted tax rates became a much more important predictor of revenue per pupil with reform. These results suggest that Michigan's reform plan provided much more ex ante fiscal neutrality than did its foundation plan.

The relationships between adjusted tax rates and adjusted wealth and household income were largely unaffected by reform.

WINNERS AND LOSERS

Table 7–5 presents, for each variable of interest, ratios of the mean for students below the median on a district characteristic to that for students above. These data suggest that reform has had no effect on the distributions of revenues among various kinds of districts. The kinds of districts that had higher per-pupil revenues before reform— the larger, the more urban, the less prone to poverty—still have them afterward. Even the magnitudes of the ratios remain virtually unchanged over the five years.

One important shift has occurred in the distributions of tax rates. Districts with a low incidence of poverty had tax rates 18 percent greater than the rates levied by more poverty-prone districts. By 1975, reform had narrowed that disparity to only 11 percent. Otherwise, the smaller and the less urban districts had substantially lower (8 to 13 percent) tax rates both before and after reform. Tax rates differed little among districts serving various proportions of minority populations.

SUMMARY AND CONCLUSIONS

Revenue disparities are generally about the same in both prereform and postreform years, but disparities in adjusted tax rates declined substantially.

With regard to fiscal neutrality, the results are mixed. The postreform years have seen much more income neutrality and substantial increases in the degree to which revenues depend on the adjusted tax rate. But wealth neutrality appears greater only in comparison with

Table 7–5. Distribution of Revenues, Instructional Expenditures, and Adjusted Tax Rates by District Characteristic: Michigan Districts, 1971–75.

	Ratio of Mean for Students below Median to Mean for Students above Median				
District Characteristic	1971 –72	1972 –73	1973 –74	1974 –75	1975 –76
General revenue					
Size	0.92	0.95	0.91	0.92	0.92
% urban	0.92	0.95	0.89	0.90	0.90
% white	1.01	0.97	1.02	1.00	1.00
% poverty	1.09	1.14	1.08	1.09	1.09
General + PL 874 revenue					
Size	0.90	0.93	0.90	0.91	0.91
% urban	0.90	0.93	0.88	0.88	0.88
% white	1.04	1.00	1.04	1.03	1.03
% poverty	1.06	1.10	1.05	1.06	1.06
Local + state revenue					
Size	0.90	0.93	0.89	0.90	0.89
% urban	0.89	0.92	0.88	0.88	0.87
% white	1.05	1.01	1.06	1.05	1.04
% poverty	1.05	1.08	1.03	1.03	1.05
Local + state + PL 874 revenue					
Size	0.88	0.91	0.89	0.89	0.88
% urban	0.88	0.91	0.86	0.87	0.86
% white	1.08	1.04	1.08	1.07	1.07
% poverty	1.02	1.05	1.01	1.01	1.02
Total revenue					
Size	0.87	0.89	0.87	0.87	0.86
% urban	0.86	0.89	0.85	0.84	0.84
% white	1.12	1.07	1.11	1.11	1.10
% poverty	0.98	1.01	0.97	0.97	0.98
Adjusted tax rates					
Size	0.88	0.92	0.87	0.88	0.88
% urban	0.89	0.93	0.86	0.86	0.87
% white	0.99	0.93	1.01	1.02	1.01
% poverty	1.18	1.26	1.14	1.11	1.11

1971. Compared with 1972, there has been little improvement in wealth neutrality.

Finally, reform has had little effect on the distribution of revenues among various kinds of districts or on the distributions of tax rates between large and small, urban and nonurban, and disproportionately white and disproportionately nonwhite districts. Districts with a low incidence of poverty levied considerably lower taxes before reform; after reform, they still levied lower taxes, but their relative advantage had been much reduced.

What did not happen in Michigan as a result of reform is as interesting as what did. Michigan's reform plan places no restrictions on districts' choices of budget levels (and tax rates). Districts in which "tastes" for education are high compared to other public and private goods and services can levy high local taxes and generate high revenues. Districts whose citizens prefer lower taxes (and lower school budgets) can indulge those desires. Despite its lack of constraints, Michigan's reform plan has not produced a wide array of district choices. If anything, the revenues are somewhat more equally distributed after reform than they were before, and disparities in local tax rates have been substantially reduced.

The distributions of revenues remain fiscally biased ex post, but that comes as no surprise. The state's guarantee extends only to the first 22 mills (in 1973) or 25 mills (in 1974) or 27 mills (in 1975). Districts are on their own thereafter and wealthier districts earn more for each mill above the matching limit than do less wealthy districts. This alone would impart some degree of wealth bias. More important, wealth was an important determinant of revenues in the prereform years. The wealthier districts had generally higher revenues and lower tax rates than the less wealthy districts. School districts tend to cut back on their budgets only in extreme circumstances; consequently, in the postreform years, the wealthier districts have tended to select tax rates that allow them to maintain previous spending levels. At the same time, there are practical limits to the rate at which a school district can utilize new resources. The less wealthy districts have increased their budgets, but at a relatively controlled rate.

In sum, Michigan's reform brought about relatively little change, not because the plan is ineffective, but rather because districts' responses to the plan have been conservative.[1]

[1]Econometric studies of Michigan school districts' behavior (Park and Carroll 1979, 1982) also conclude that the guaranteed tax base (GTB) plan did not increase expenditures appreciably.

8 THE EFFECTS OF REFORM IN NEW MEXICO

This chapter reviews New Mexico's prereform and postreform school finance systems, describes the data available for the analysis, and identifies the effects of reform. The analysis concentrates on the consequences of reform for the distributions of revenues per pupil, instructional expenditures per pupil, and adjusted tax rates, for fiscal neutrality, and for various kinds of districts. The chapter ends with a summary of our findings and conclusions.

SCHOOL FINANCE IN NEW MEXICO

New Mexico changed its school finance plan in 1974. Before then, most state aid was distributed through four major programs: the basic program, supplemental distributions, special education, and transportation. There were other, less important, state distributions for vocational education and emergency aid. The state also funded all textbooks.

The basic program employed a staffing formula whereby a district was allocated a number of staff positions in each of thirteen professional and nonprofessional staff categories according to its average daily membership (ADM) (e.g., one principal for each 400 pupils). The staff allocations were then multiplied by a legislatively deter-

Table 8–1. Summary of New Mexico Districts (dollar amounts in thousands).

Item	1972–73	1973–74	1974–75	1975–76
Number of districts	88	88	88	88
Assessed valuation	2,789,599	3,050,079	3,430,316	3,745,720
Average daily membership	276,155	273,743	273,063	265,374
Revenue				
Federal	45,183	42,349	47,524	56,368
State	162,234	177,351	202,410	231,265
County	30,354	30,011		
Local	51,432	67,107	97,322	106,620
Total, all sources	279,203	308,818	347,256	394,253

mined appropriation unit for each category (e.g., $13,085 per principal in 1973); 25 percent of the sum across categories was added for support costs. The state funded 70 percent of the total.

The supplemental distributions included a small equalization aid program (essentially a foundation plan), which was about 8 percent of the basic program's size; programs that covered isolated and essential schools (eight districts); program enrichment (nine districts); emergency distributions; and out-of-state tuition, when it was not feasible for students to attend a New Mexico school district. The state paid the cost of special education at a fixed rate based on the number of special education pupils (school-aged physically or mentally handicapped). This distribution was approximately $1,000 per special education ADM. The actual distribution was based on a formula for the number of teachers and support costs required.

The state paid the total approved transportation costs. The district transportation plan was approved by the state transportation director. The minimum distances were 1 mile for grades 1–6, 1.5 miles for grades 7–9, and 2 miles for grades 10–12, except where walking conditions were hazardous.

School districts still order all their new textbooks through the state. As the requisitions are approved, the state purchases the books from mineral lease income.

Local revenues made up only a small percentage of New Mexico school districts' total revenues. (See Table 8–1 for a summary of New Mexico districts and their revenues by source.) The maximum district tax rate was 4.45 mills except in municipalities, where it was 2.225 mills, unless the municipality waived part of its levy to the school district. No specific district tax was required for participation in state support programs. Nearly all school district tax rates were at a minimum limit.

New Mexico had a county school tax levy. The proceeds were distributed by the county superintendent to all school districts with territory within the county. The tax rate was fixed at 6.7 mills, unless county reappraisals were not completed; then the rate was 5.0 mills. The county school tax levy was distributed to districts based on their share of total county ADM. Districts that crossed county boundaries received a share based on the ADM that resided in each of the counties.

Under the accounting system used at the time, income from motor vehicle license fees was also reported as county income. County superintendents were responsible for distributing to school districts a portion of the state-collected motor vehicle license fees. District shares were determined by shares of ADM.

Federal funds accounted for less than 20 percent of the funds available for all school districts in 1972–73, but were an important part of total revenue in selected individual school districts. Federal impact aid [Public Law (PL) 874] was received by fifty-seven of New Mexico's eighty-eight school districts. The largest recipients were Albuquerque, Gallup, and Alamagordo, which received nearly one-half of the state total funds under PL 874. In Albuquerque, PL 874 contributed 6 percent of the total budget; in Gallup, 25 percent; and in Alamagordo, 20 percent. Atomic Energy Commission funds are received by one New Mexico district, Los Alamos, where they make up nearly 40 percent (and impact aid another 10 percent) of the district's total revenues. This contribution is based on the presence of the Los Alamos Laboratory of the Atomic Energy Commission. Forest Reserve funds are received by county treasurers based on the presence of federal Forest Reserve lands; twenty-two of New Mexico's thirty-two counties receive these funds and distribute them to fifty-six districts according to their share of the county's ADM. The Johnson-O'Malley Act was passed in 1934 to assist public schools financially where they serve large blocks of Indian students or contain large tracts of Indian children. Since 1950, with the passage of PL 874, Johnson-O'Malley funds have been used for the special needs of Indian children. Twenty New Mexico districts received Johnson-O'Malley funds; the largest share (nearly one-third) went to the Gallup district.

The New Mexico school finance reform of 1974 (House Bill 85) abolished a statewide local property tax rate of 8.925 mills. This rate is equal to the sum of the county rate and the municipal maximum rate before reform.

The state contribution formula is based on a weighted student characteristics index, which is intended to measure cost differentials for the educational program needs of different categories of students. The state fixes a price per program unit; multiplying that price by the total weighted units for a school district yields the district's total educational need. Sources of funds are subtracted from the need to compute the state equalization guarantee.

Calculation of need was based on pupil cost differentials in the revised formula. Weights were established as follows:

- Regular categories of students: kindergarten (early childhood education), grades 1–3, grades 4–6, grades 7–9, grades 10–12.
- Special categories of students: special education C (moderately handicapped), special education D (severely handicapped).
- As add-ons for the following programs: vocational, bilingual/multicultural, special education A/B (itinerant teacher/resource room).

The number of students in each category is multiplied by the category weight to get the weighted number of students. For students in vocational or bilingual/multicultural programs, the number of full-time equivalents (FTE) in the program is multiplied by the program add-on factor to get the weighted program units. For special education A and B programs, the number of programs is multiplied by the weight of the programs to get weighted program units. The sum of the weighted number of students and the weighted program units for all special educational programs is the total weighted program units.

These program units are adjusted by an index of teacher training and experience, which is calculated for each district. The index is derived from a table of weights for five categories of years of experience and five categories of level of experience. The number of teachers in each cell is multiplied by the cell weight to give the weighted teachers. The sum of the weighted teachers is divided by the actual total number of teachers to obtain the index of teacher training and experience. This index is multiplied by the total pupil program units to obtain the adjusted program units.

The resources available to pay for need are computed as 95 percent of the sum of the following funds:

- Proceeds from the 8.925-mill levy in the districts.
- District's share of motor vehicle license fees.
- Federal PL 874 revenues to the district.
- Federal Forest Reserve distributions to the district.
- Regular federal vocational program revenues.

The total of these funds available to the district is obtained from the program cost to find the state equalization guarantee.

The state continues to fund 100 percent of approved transportation costs. The supplemental distribution includes out-of-state tuition, emergency aid, and funds for program enrichment. Instead of a special program for isolated schools, a sparsity factor was included in calculating the equalization grant. Special education and vocational aid were also included in the equalization program as add-on costs for computing need.

In 1975, state aid to school districts was expanded to include a capital outlay assistance program (Senate Bill 9). Districts that levied a 1-mill or 2-mill tax for capital improvements for a period up to a maximum of three years were entitled to the difference between $35 per mill and the local yield from this fund.

DATA AND DEFINITIONS

We obtained data on New Mexico districts' revenues, expenditures, and assessed values from the Intercultural Development Research Association for the 1972–73 through 1975–76 school years. Finance data for those years were available for all eighty-eight districts. Census data were available for sixty-eight of the districts, which served about 272,000 students in 1972, and 261,000 in 1975.

In the prereform years of 1972 and 1973, general revenue included all local revenues, the district's receipts from the general county school tax and from motor vehicle license fees, and its receipts from the state basic program. Our data exclude the proceeds from local property taxes that are levied for debt service interest and principal. We treat all other revenues from state sources as state categorical revenues. Federal revenues included revenues from federal programs paid into the operational fund and all revenues from federal sources paid into the federal projects fund. Office of Economic Opportunity (OEO) funds (e.g., Headstart, Neighborhood Youth Corps, the Day Care Community Action Program) are excluded.

New Mexico assesses property at one-third market value. Assessment sales ratios are developed in special studies of property assessment ratios by county. We adjust each district's assessed value and district tax rate (plus the general county school tax rate in the prereform years) by the assessment sales ratio for its primary county.

The same definitions are used in the postreform years, 1974 and 1975. The only differences are the elimination of the county school foundation fund and the general county school tax.

THE DISTRIBUTION OF REVENUES, INSTRUCTIONAL EXPENDITURES, AND ADJUSTED TAX RATES

Table 8–2 shows the mean, coefficient of variation, median, and relative deviation from the median for the distribution of per-pupil revenues at five levels of aggregation, instructional expenditures per pupil, and adjusted tax rates. It is apparent that reform was accompanied by a very substantial increase in general revenues per pupil. Between 1973 and 1974, these revenues grew by about $209—over seven times the $28 increase realized in the last year before reform; and the second year of reform saw a further increase of $102 per pupil.

New Mexico's plan attempts to equalize impact aid receipts. Judged on those terms, it has been very successful; coefficients of variation for the distribution of general plus PL 874 revenue per pupil dropped sharply when the reform plan was introduced. The relative deviation from the median exhibits even greater declines between the prereform years of 1972 and 1973, and the postreform years of 1974 and 1975.

The effect of including PL 874 funds in the equalization target can be seen by comparing the results for general revenue per pupil with those for general plus PL 874 revenue per pupil. Note that the coefficients of variation and relative deviations from the median were about 3 percentage points higher for the latter in the prereform years. Moreover, if the reform plan had not deducted impact aid in apportioning state general aid, each district would have received additional state

Table 8–2. Measures of the Distribution of Revenues, Instructional Expenditures, and Adjusted Tax Rates: New Mexico Districts, 1972–75.

Measure	1972–73	1973–74	1974–75	1975–76
General revenue				
Mean	580	608	817	919
Coefficient of variation	0.14	0.15	0.15	0.16
Median	558	582	832	944
Relative deviation	0.07	0.08	0.09	0.09
General + PL 874 revenue				
Mean	650	659	873	983
Coefficient of variation	0.17	0.18	0.12	0.10
Median	609	611	866	975
Relative deviation	0.10	0.11	0.06	0.05
Local + state revenue				
Mean	711	789	892	1,006
Coefficient of variation	0.14	0.19	0.19	0.17
Median	669	737	876	999
Relative deviation	0.09	0.10	0.10	0.09
Local + state + PL 874 revenue				
Mean	781	839	947	1,070
Coefficient of variation	0.15	0.18	0.17	0.14
Median	713	782	910	1030
Relative deviation	0.10	0.10	0.08	0.07
Total revenue				
Mean	862	929	1,035	1,184
Coefficient of variation	0.19	0.22	0.19	0.17
Median	781	834	950	1,087
Relative deviation	0.13	0.15	0.12	0.10
Instructional expenditures				
Mean	512	551	614	709
Coefficient of variation	0.11	0.11	0.10	0.09
Median	492	528	613	709
Relative deviation	0.06	0.06	0.05	0.05
Adjusted tax rates				
Mean	3.9	3.7	3.7	3.0
Coefficient of variation	0.29	0.31	0.10	0.00
Median	4.0	3.7	3.7	3.0
Relative deviation	0.18	0.18	0.06	0.00

Note: All revenue measures and instructional expenditures are dollars per pupil. Adjusted tax rates are mills.

general aid equal to its PL 874 revenues; the distributions of general revenue per pupil in the postreform years would have equaled what were the distributions of general plus PL 874 revenue per pupil. The coefficients of variation for general revenue per pupil then would have been 0.12 in 1974 and 0.10 in 1975, and the relative deviations from the median would have been 0.06 and 0.05 in the same two years. The change in the basic structure of New Mexico's finance system, aside from inclusion of PL 874 revenue in the equalization target, thus appears to be responsible for declines of about 3 percentage points (or 20 percent) in the coefficient of variation for general revenue per pupil, and about 2 percentage points (or 20 percent) in the relative deviations from the median.

The postreform drop in the coefficient of variation for the distribution of general plus PL 874 revenue per pupil is about 6.5 percentage points. If we assume that roughly 3 of those points can be attributed to reform of the finance system's basic structure, New Mexico's approach to equalizing PL 874 revenues resulted in a decline of about 3.5 percentage points in the coefficient of variation for the distribution of general plus PL 874 revenue per pupil. This interpretation of the results is consistent with our earlier observation that, in the prereform years, PL 874 revenues accounted for about 3 percentage points in the coefficients of variation and relative deviations from the median for the distribution of general plus PL 874 revenues per pupil.

New Mexico folded some of its categorical programs into the state general aid formula when it adopted a pupil-weighting system. Categorical revenue per pupil fell from $131 in 1972 and $181 in 1973 to $75 in 1974 and $85 in 1975. More to the point, the distribution of state categorical aid is highly disequalizing in the postreform years. The coefficients of variation for the distribution of local plus state PL 874 revenue per pupil are 4 to 5 percentage points above the comparable statistics for the distribution of general plus PL 874 revenue per pupil in 1974 and 1975. Similarly, in the postreform years, the relative deviation from the median for the former are about one-third greater than those for the latter.

Federal categorical revenues also boost the coefficients of variation and relative deviations from the median in the postreform years. (Compare the results for the local plus state plus PL 874 revenue per pupil with those for per-pupil total revenue.)

Instructional expenditures per pupil exhibit the patterns we observed in the other states: They are more equally distributed than any other revenue variable in every year, and their distribution is much less sensitive to reform than are the revenue distributions.

Reform brought about sharp declines in adjusted tax rates. Moreover, by the second year of reform, every district was levying the state-mandated 8.925 mills. Complete equality in tax rates has been achieved.

WEALTH, INCOME, AND TAX NEUTRALITY

Table 8–3 presents the elasticities, at the mean, implied by quadratic regressions of per-pupil revenues, at five levels of aggregation, instructional expenditures per pupil, and adjusted tax rates.

Wealth has been an extremely important determinant of general revenues per pupil in the prereform years. Reform does not reduce the degrees to which revenues per pupil depend on wealth except in the case of total revenues in 1975, where the regression is not significant at the 10 percent level.

Household income per pupil, which had been an insignificant predictor of general revenues per pupil before reform, became a significant determinant of that variable by the second year of reform. Conversely, per-pupil revenues at higher levels of aggregation became less significantly related to income after reform. Finally, total revenue per pupil was significantly related to income in all four years.

Adjusted tax rates were not significantly related to general revenues per pupil before reform. The transitional year, 1974, saw a significant association between the two variables, but New Mexico's plan precludes a continuing relationship in the postreform era.

The elasticities of revenues per pupil with respect to wealth dropped sharply with reform. Corresponding elasticities with respect to income were generally negligible before the reform and are always negligible after. The elasticities of revenues with respect to the tax rate are forced to zero by the reform plan.

Instructional expenditures per pupil are significantly related to both wealth and income in both prereform and postreform years. There are no changes in the elasticity of instructional expenditures with respect to either income or wealth. Instructional expenditures per pupil had

Table 8–3. Elasticity of Revenues, Instructional Expenditures, and Adjusted Tax Rates with Respect to Adjusted Wealth, Household Income, and Adjusted Tax Rates: New Mexico Districts, 1972–75.

Dependent/Independent Variable	1972–73	1973–74	1974–75	1975–76
General revenue				
Adjusted wealth	0.176	0.193	0.108	0.043
Household income	0.068	0.104	0.052	0.089
Adjusted tax rate	0.143	−0.082	0.368	0.000
General + PL 874 revenue				
Adjusted wealth	0.147	0.179	0.102	0.046
Household income	0.044	0.017	0.001	0.000
Adjusted tax rate	0.306	−0.217	0.201	0.000
Local + state revenue				
Adjusted wealth	0.106	0.075	0.104	0.053
Household income	0.093	−0.119	−0.047	0.008
Adjusted tax rate	0.149	−0.016	0.365	0.000
Local + state + PL 874 revenue				
Adjusted wealth	0.088	0.071	0.099	0.055
Household income	0.171	−0.173	−0.089	−0.068
Adjusted tax rate	0.284	−0.127	0.211	0.000
Total revenue				
Adjusted wealth	0.061	0.044	0.080	0.024
Household income	0.080	−0.124	−0.036	−0.017
Adjusted tax rate	0.329	−0.165	0.073	0.000
Instructional expenditures				
Adjusted wealth	0.058	0.046	0.047	0.045
Household income	0.180	0.177	0.198	0.209
Adjusted tax rate	0.187	−0.143	0.014	0.000
Adjusted tax rates				
Adjusted wealth	0.252	−0.223	−0.001	0.000
Household income	0.094	−0.142	0.057	0.000

been significantly related to adjusted tax rates before reform. Reform eliminated that relationship.

By 1975, all New Mexico districts levied the mandated nominal local property tax rate of 8.925 mills. Obviously, tax rates are equal across districts and entirely independent of adjusted wealth, household income, and other district characteristics.

WINNERS AND LOSERS

Table 8–4 shows that New Mexico's reform has affected the distribution of general revenues per pupil among different kinds of districts. The smaller districts (below the median ADM) had 10 to 12 percent more general revenue per pupil before reform, but now have only about 4 percent more. The less urban districts averaged about 5 percent more general revenue per pupil before reform; by 1975 they averaged nearly 5 percent less. Relative general revenue per pupil fell by roughly 5 percentage points in disproportionately nonwhite districts and fell 2 or 3 percentage points in districts serving a relatively large poverty population.

The distribution of general plus PL 874 revenue among different kinds of districts is generally the same as was observed for general revenue per pupil. The major exception is that, compared with districts serving above-median percentages of white populations, those serving more minority populations had about 7 percent greater general plus PL 874 revenue per pupil before reform and about 1 percent less after. These districts had about 4 percent less general revenue per pupil before reform and nearly 10 percent less after reform. Reform has not changed the distributional pattern, but PL 874 revenue has "compensated" minority districts for their general revenue deficiencies.

In the prereform years, the smaller districts, the more rural, the more white, and the more poverty-prone tended to receive greater local plus state revenue per pupil. The smaller and more rural districts have retained their relative advantage, but reform has narrowed the differences between them and the larger and more urban districts. Districts serving large minority populations have lost local plus state revenue per pupil compared with districts serving large white populations. Reform has eliminated the advantage once held by poverty-prone districts.

Before reform, the smaller districts had averaged about 15 percent more local plus state plus PL 874 revenue per pupil compared with districts above the median in size. Reform seems to have reduced that advantage, and also that of the more rural districts. Districts serving more disproportionately nonwhite populations not only lost their advantage with reform, but surrendered it to the white districts. The prereform advantage of poverty-prone districts was somewhat reduced.

Table 8–4. Distribution of Revenues, Instructional Expenditures, and Adjusted Tax Rates by District Characteristic: New Mexico Districts, 1972–75.

	Ratio of Mean for Students below Median to Mean for Students above Median			
District Characteristic	1972–73	1973–74	1974–75	1975–76
General revenue				
Size	1.10	1.12	1.05	1.04
% urban	1.05	1.06	1.00	0.96
% white	0.96	0.96	0.91	0.90
% poverty	1.03	1.03	1.04	1.06
General + PL 874 revenue				
Size	1.09	1.12	1.06	1.05
% urban	1.09	1.10	1.04	1.01
% white	1.08	1.06	0.99	0.98
% poverty	0.98	0.99	1.00	1.01
Local + state revenue				
Size	1.14	1.16	1.11	1.09
% urban	1.09	1.12	1.06	1.02
% white	0.95	0.94	0.91	0.90
% poverty	0.95	0.93	0.98	1.00
Local + state + PL 874 revenue				
Size	1.13	1.15	1.11	1.09
% urban	1.12	1.15	1.09	1.06
% white	1.05	1.01	0.97	0.97
% poverty	0.92	0.91	0.95	0.96
Total revenue				
Size	1.16	1.21	1.17	1.14
% urban	1.16	1.21	1.14	1.11
% white	1.04	1.01	0.97	0.96
% poverty	0.89	0.86	0.91	0.91
Instructional expenditures				
Size	1.07	1.06	1.04	1.04
% urban	1.02	1.02	0.99	0.97
% white	1.00	1.00	0.98	0.97
% poverty	1.01	1.00	1.04	1.04
Adjusted tax rates				
Size	1.07	1.16	0.97	1.00
% urban	1.03	1.08	0.97	1.00
% white	1.17	1.18	1.04	1.00
% poverty	0.99	0.98	1.05	1.00

In terms of total revenue per pupil, the smaller, the more rural, and the minority districts are the big losers in New Mexico. The smaller and more rural districts had an advantage of 16 to 20 percent before reform; it declined to 10 to 14 percent by 1975. Minority districts averaged about 4 percent greater per-pupil total revenues in 1972, but about 4 percent less by 1975. The distribution of total revenues per pupil between more and less poverty-prone populations has changed little with reform.

Reform appears to have had little effect on the distribution of total expenditures among different types of districts. There has been a mild shift from slightly higher instructional expenditures in the more rural districts to slightly higher ones in the more urban districts. Otherwise, reform has brought about few changes.

As for adjusted local property tax rates, the more rural and the more minority districts gained on their counterparts: The rates tended to be higher in those districts after reform.

Reform roughly equalized the average tax rates between more and less poverty-prone districts.

SUMMARY AND CONCLUSIONS

All in all, New Mexico's reform appears to have had surprisingly little effect on the distributions of per-pupil revenues and instructional expenditures, and on the relationships between those variables and districts' characteristics.

Disparities in general revenue per pupil, in local plus state revenue per pupil, and in instructional expenditures per pupil have not been reduced at all. Disparities in local plus PL 874 revenue per pupil, in local plus state plus PL 874 revenue per pupil, and in total revenue per pupil have been somewhat reduced, but the reductions in disparities in the latter two variables are small. It appears that reform's primary effect, as far as distributional equality is concerned, has been to equalize PL 874 revenues.

Fiscal neutrality has generally improved in New Mexico, but adjusted wealth remains a significant predictor of all five revenue measures and of instructional expenditures. Reform has improved income neutrality with regard to some measures, but other measures have become more closely related to income. Per-pupil general revenue, total revenue, and instructional expenditures tend to be significantly higher in the higher income districts. Per-pupil general plus PL 874 revenue, local plus state revenue, and local plus state plus PL 874 revenue are independent of household income per pupil. All variables depended on adjusted tax rates before reform; those relationships have been fully eliminated by reform.

The larger districts, the more urban, and the more white have gained on their counterparts, but their gains have been small. The larger and the more urban districts still have lower average revenues and instructional expenditures. After reform, average revenues and expenditures in the more minority districts were generally lower than in the white districts. The reverse had been true before reform. However, none of these shifts have been very large.

These results are quite surprising. After all, New Mexico's pre-reform plan essentially provided flat grants per student. And flat-grant systems are, at best, only mildly equalizing and do nothing to offset the fiscal advantages of wealthier and higher income districts. The state shifted to a plan that closely approximates full state assumption. Districts must levy the mandated property tax rate. Their revenue needs are determined by formula. And the state makes up the difference between the formula-determined revenue needs and the proceeds of the local tax levy. Why, then, did a shift from the most mildly equalizing of state aid plans to one that fully funds revenue needs fail to bring about greater equality? And how is it that a plan that precludes local discretion regarding tax rates and revenue needs should fail to achieve fiscal neutrality and should allow (some) revenues and instructional expenditures to vary with income?

We suspect that the answers lie in the adjustment factor for teachers' experience and education. Prior to reform, some New Mexico districts took advantage of their fiscal opportunities and raised greater per-pupil revenues than did other districts. They were then able to employ more highly educated and experienced teachers than the lower wealth districts could afford. Their teachers' experience and education index was, accordingly, relatively high in the postreform years, raising their revenue entitlements according to the formula.

Because the data we obtained did not provide information on that factor, we could not explicitly test this hypothesis, but it is consistent with the available data. Note also that this feature of New Mexico's plan tends to "lock-in" revenue disparities whether or not they are associated with wealth. A district that enters the reform era with a highly educated and experienced staff will enjoy a high adjustment factor and therefore high revenues with which it can retain such a staff. The opposite is true for a district with a less qualified staff: The plan would perpetuate its inability to afford highly qualified new teachers. Assuming that teacher education and experience directly affect the quality of instruction, the plan thus appears to work against reform's ultimate objective: reducing interdistrict disparities in the quality of education offered to children.

9 INTERSTATE COMPARISONS AND CONCLUSIONS

The following review discusses similarities and differences among the five states' experience with reform, presents our general conclusions, and speculates on why these reforms yielded the outcomes they did. We focus on how reform affected the distributions of three variables: general plus Public Law (PL) 874 revenues per pupil, instructional expenditures per pupil, and adjusted tax rates. The distributions of the other revenue variables resemble those of general plus PL 874 revenue per pupil and suggest the same conclusions.

THE EFFECTS OF REFORM ON REVENUES, SPENDING, AND TAX RATES

Table 9–1 presents revenues per pupil, instructional expenditures per pupil, and adjusted tax rates for each state in each year. The results support three conclusions:

- Reform has generally been accompanied by substantial increases in revenues per pupil.
- Reform has generally been accompanied by somewhat smaller increases in instructional expenditures per pupil.

151

Table 9–1. Revenues per Pupil, Instructional Expenditures per Pupil, and Adjusted Tax Rates.

	Prereform			Postreform			
State and Variable	1970–71	1971–72	1972–73	1973–74	1974–75	1975–76	1976–77
Revenues							
California							
Elementary	745	780	860	999	1,076	1,196	1,327
High school	1,007	1,058	1,148	1,230	1,274	1,388	1,519
Unified	825	882	992	1,078	1,162	1,277	1,412
Florida			815			1,149	
Kansas							
ADM below 400			1,200	1,274	1,488		
ADM 400 to 1,299			881	996	1,119		
ADM 1,300 and above			772	907	1,035		
Michigan		845	901	1,014	1,123	1,242	
New Mexico			650	659	874	983	
Instructional							
expenditures							
California							
Elementary	553	591	634	717	684	746	821
High School	723	769	809	869	781	830	899
Unified	628	665	712	792	715	757	833
Florida			625			853	
Kansas							
ADM below 400			746	761	848		
ADM 400 to 1,299			595	621	688		
ADM 1,300 and above			563	575	643		
New Mexico			512	551	614	709	
Adjusted tax rates							
California							
Elementary	7.2	7.4	7.6	6.7	6.7	7.0	6.9
High School	5.6	5.7	6.0	5.3	5.2	5.5	5.4
Unified	11.3	11.8	12.1	11.1	11.6	11.8	11.7
Florida			8.1			6.5	
Kansas							
ADM below 400			5.0	5.7	5.9		
ADM 400 to 1,299			5.8	5.4	6.0		
ADM 1,300 and above			8.1	7.4	7.7		
Michigan		12.3	12.1	12.7	13.2	13.6	
New Mexico			3.9	3.7	3.7	3.0	

Note: Instructional expenditures were unavailable for Michigan. California eliminated its instructional expenditures compilation in 1975–76. We aggregated the accounts that had been included in instructional expenditures prior to then; the 1975–76 drop in per-pupil instructional expenditures in all three types of California districts probably reflects some difference between our calculation and the procedure California had used to calculate instructional expenditures. All results are based on student-weighted observations.

• Most tax rates dropped in the first year of reform, several of them substantially, and often remained lower for several years.

In all five states, the postreform years saw impressive revenue growth, not all of which is solely attributable to reform, however. The states probably would have increased school revenues anyway, though probably not as much as they did under the stimulus of reform. Prior to reform, for example, California elementary, high school, and unified district revenues per pupil grew at average annual rates of 7.7 percent, 7.0 percent, and 10.1 percent. The comparable rates after reform were 13.6, 8.1, and 10.6. The differences between prereform and postreform average annual revenue growth rates are dramatic in Michigan—6.6 percent as against 12.6 percent—and even more so in New Mexico—1.3 percent as against 24.6 percent. We lacked the data to perform similar comparisons for Florida and Kansas districts. Postreform average annual growth rates in revenues were 13.7 percent in Florida and ranged from 12.0 percent (small districts) to 17.0 percent (large districts) in Kansas. The credit must go to reform. In the ordinary course of events, state legislatures are not given to sudden bursts of munificence.

The postreform growth in revenues per pupil is even more impressive in view of the sharp drop in many school tax rates in the first year of reform. Tax rates rose after reform only in Michigan and in Kansas's small and medium districts.

The results for Michigan are particularly interesting. Michigan imposed no limits on school districts' revenues or taxes, but neither one increased dramatically. Nor did the shift from the foundation plan lead districts to cut their spending or even fail to keep pace with the rates of growth in revenues in other states.

Neglecting the California data, instructional expenditures per pupil have grown in every state in every year, but their rate of growth is lower in every case than the rate of growth of revenues. The same is true for all three types of California districts in the prereform years and over the 1974–75 to 1976–77 period. It seems to be generally true, then, that when school districts receive increases in per-pupil revenues, they do not make proportional increases in their instructional expenditures per pupil.

Table 9–2.   Coefficients of Variation for Revenues, Instructional Expenditures, and Adjusted Tax Rates.

State and Variable	Prereform			Postreform			
	1970—71	1971–72	1972–73	1973–74	1974–75	1975–76	1976–77
Revenues							
California							
Elementary	0.22	0.23	0.22	0.21	0.20	0.18	0.18
High school	0.17	0.18	0.18	0.19	0.17	0.17	0.16
Unified	0.18	0.19	0.18	0.16	0.14	0.14	0.13
Florida			0.12			0.13	
Kansas							
ADM below 400			0.23	0.21	0.22		
ADM 400 to 1,299			0.21	0.18	0.20		
ADM 1,300 and above			0.12	0.11	0.10		
Michigan		0.15	0.17	0.15	0.14	0.16	
New Mexico			0.17	0.18	0.12	0.10	
Instructional expenditures							
California							
Elementary	0.17	0.17	0.17	0.16	0.18	0.16	0.15
High school	0.14	0.15	0.15	0.14	0.16	0.15	0.14
Unified	0.17	0.17	0.18	0·17	0.18	0.15	0.13
Florida			0.12			0.14	
Kansas							
ADM below 400			0.21	0.21	0.20		
ADM 400 to 1,299			0.19	0.17	0.19		
ADM 1,300 and above			0.11	0.09	0.09		
New Mexico			0.11	0.11	0.10	0.09	
Adjusted tax rates							
California							
Elementary	0.22	0.23	0.23	0.22	0.17	0.17	0.17
High school	0.17	0.17	0.17	0.15	0.13	0.14	0.14
Unified	0.17	0.16	0.17	0.15	0.14	0.13	0.12
Florida			0.11			0.10	
Kansas							
ADM below 400			0.28	0.20	0.19		
ADM 400 to 1,299			0.28	0.23	0.18		
ADM 1,300 and above			0.22	0.23	0.15		
Michigan		0.20	0.24	0.18	0.15	0.14	
New Mexico			0.29	0.31	0.10	0.00	

THE EFFECTS OF REFORM ON
DISTRIBUTIONAL EQUALITY

Table 9–2 presents coefficients of variation for per-pupil distributions of revenues, instructional expenditures, and adjusted tax rates.[1] The results suggest three conclusions:

- Reform efforts in these five states have brought about somewhat more equal distributions of per-pupil revenues.
- Reform has done little, if anything, to reduce disparities in instructional expenditures per pupil in any of the five states.
- Reform has generally led to more equal distributions of adjusted tax rates.

The Distribution of Revenues Per Pupil

Revenue disparities among California's unified districts and among New Mexico's districts dropped sharply with reform. Roughly half the decline observed in New Mexico reflects the new treatment of PL 874 revenue; the other half is due to the state's virtually complete assumption of school finance responsibilities.

Smaller improvements in per-pupil revenue distribution are found in California's elementary districts and in Kansas's larger districts. Reform has had little effect in California's high school districts, in Florida, in Kansas's smaller and medium-sized districts, and in Michigan.

To be sure, Florida and New Mexico attempted to equalize cost-adjusted and need-adjusted distributions of revenues, and Michigan did not address the revenue equalization issue. Nonetheless, their revenue distributions remained about what they were; and as we shall see below, the same kinds of districts are found in the upper and lower

---

[1] A commonly used distributional index, the coefficient of variation, is the standard deviation divided by the mean. A value of, say, 0.22 means that approximately two-thirds of the students in a state attend districts where revenues (instructional expenditures, tax rates) are within 22 percent of the mean, and about one-sixth where revenues are more than 22 percent below the mean, and about one-sixth where revenues are 22 percent above the mean. Thus, a reduction in the coefficient from one year to the next implies that districts are, on average, relatively closer to the mean in the second year; that is, the distribution has become more equal.

portions of the distribution. In each of these states, the districts that had higher revenues before reform also had them afterward.

It may be that a distribution of revenues is "inequitable" when it stems from one finance system and is "equitable," or at least less inequitable, when it stems from another. But most of the arguments put forward by reform proponents suggest that the distribution itself is at issue. From that perspective, only New Mexico and California, in its unified districts, have approached true equity. The other states have changed the rules whereby districts raise local revenues and receive state general aid, but they have not much changed the consequences.

The Distribution of Instructional Expenditures Per Pupil

The distribution of instructional expenditures per pupil has changed but little in spite of sharp rises in revenues. The coefficient of variation falls a point or two in some cases and grows a point or two in others, but there are no impressive changes in either direction.

It is interesting that, both before and after reform, the coefficients of variation for the distributions of instructional expenditures per pupil are smaller than those for the corresponding distributions of revenues per pupil. These results, like those reported earlier for reform's effects on levels of revenues and expenditures, imply that districts with abundant revenues spend a large share of them for noninstructional purposes. Furthermore, in those cases where the coefficient of variation for per-pupil revenues declined, there were smaller declines in the corresponding coefficient of variation for instructional expenditures. This reinforces our earlier conjecture that, when reform substantially increases a previously low-spending district's revenues, it tends to put those funds to noninstructional uses. These results are consistent with previous studies of school district behavior (Alexander 1974; Barro and Carroll 1975; Carroll 1976) which found that as districts' per-pupil budgets increase, they allocate decreasing proportions of their budgets to expenditures for teachers.

Taken together, these observations suggest the following hypothesis: School districts generally agree on what constitutes an acceptable instructional program and exert every effort to provide one. In doing so, districts with low revenue per pupil make do with scanty noninstructional resources. When they receive budget increases, they spend a large share of the new money on "catching up" with more prosperous districts in terms of noninstructional expenditures, and a much smaller share on improving the instructional program.

What all this implies depends on one's view of the relationship between noninstructional expenditures and the objectives of reform. Some expenditures (e.g., for adult education) appear to be peripheral to the main reform themes. Others, however, may directly promote reform objectives. Improving plant operation and maintenance, for example, may be important in a district that has not had enough funds for adequate upkeep of buildings and equipment. At one extreme, if all school resources are equally important, it does not matter whether or not districts devote new revenues to instruction. At the other extreme, if educational quality is determined by instructional expenditures, and if the objective of reform is to equalize that quality for all students, then the states have increased school revenues to little avail, and the benefits have gone to the wrong people.

The Distribution of Adjusted Tax Rates

The reforms enacted by three of the five states—Kansas and Michigan are the exceptions—led to reductions in adjusted tax rates; and in every state except Florida, coefficients of variation for the distributions of adjusted tax rates fell more than 25 percent. New Mexico entirely eliminated variation in local educational property tax rates. Even in Michigan, where reform was accompanied by a roughly 6 percent increase in the weighted average adjusted tax rate, the distribution of adjusted tax rates was dramatically equalized by reform.

THE EFFECTS OF REFORM ON FISCAL NEUTRALITY

We explored the effects of each state's reform on three concepts of fiscal neutrality. Two of these concepts reflect the relationship between revenues (or expenditures) and fiscal capacity—measured alternatively by the property tax base per pupil and household income per pupil. The third reflects the relationship between revenues (or expenditures) and fiscal effort—measured by the property tax rate. In each case, we use the elasticity of revenues per pupil (or expenditures per pupil) with respect to wealth per pupil (or household income per pupil or tax rates)[2] as the measure of neutrality. Again, three conclusions can be drawn:

- Reform has improved the wealth neutrality of revenues per pupil. Instructional expenditures per pupil are generally as closely related to property tax bases after reform as they had been before.
- Although income neutrality has improved in some cases, the distributions of revenues and instructional expenditures per pupil in other cases are more income-biased than they were before. Some reforms have worsened the relationship that originally gave rise to the reform movement.
- Ex ante fiscal neutrality has improved in some cases and worsened in others.

Wealth Neutrality

A widely accepted version of the fiscal neutrality concept refers to the relationship between districts' revenues (or expenditures) and their property tax bases. Fiscal neutrality, according to this view, requires that revenues per pupil be independent of property tax bases; that is, elasticities of revenues (expenditures) with respect to wealth should equal zero.

The elasticities presented in Table 9–3 reflect that concept of fiscal neutrality. Higher elasticities imply a closer association between revenues, expenditures, or tax rates, on the other hand, and wealth, measured by the property tax base per pupil, on the other.

Reform reduced revenue elasticities (improved wealth neutrality) in California, in Kansas's large districts, and in New Mexico, but brought little or no improvement for Florida, Kansas's small and medium-sized districts, and Michigan.

As for instructional expenditures, there was some improvement in Kansas's small and medium-sized districts, but elasticities elsewhere remained about the same.

---

[2]The elasticity of one variable with respect to another is the percentage change in the first variable that, on average, is associated with a 1 percent change in the second. An elasticity of revenues with respect to wealth of 0.195 means that the average district's revenues increase by 0.195 percent with each 1 percent increase in its wealth. The elasticities reported here were obtained from quadratic regressions of revenues per pupil (or instructional expenditures per pupil) on wealth (or on household income per pupil or on tax rates).

Table 9–3. Elasticity of Revenues per Pupil and Instructional Expenditures per Pupil with Respect to Adjusted Wealth per Pupil.

	Prereform			Postreform			
State and Variable	1970–71	1971–72	1972–73	1973–74	1974–75	1975–76	1976–77
Revenues							
California							
Elementary	0.195	0.214	0.241	0.202	0.180	0.150	0.148
High school	0.380	0.399	0.396	0.388	0.329	0.331	0.307
Unified	0.289	0.320	0.332	0.250	0.236	0.203	0.205
Florida			0.199			0.214	
Kansas							
ADM below 400			0.471	0.349	0.444		
ADM 400 to 1,299			0.420	0.326	0.352		
ADM 1,300 and above			0.219	0.111	0.141		
Michigan		0.253	0.235	0.236	0.233	0.238	
New Mexico			0.147	0.179	0.102	0.046	
Instructional expenditures							
California							
Elementary	0.096	0.105	0.108	0.090	0.117	0.101	0.104
High school	0.266	0.267	0.286	0.261	0.266	0.268	0.247
Unified	0.224	0.235	0.256	0.249	0.248	0.217	0.179
Florida			0.183			0.213	
Kansas							
ADM below 400			0.381	0.371	0.328		
ADM 400 to 1,299			0.352	0.326	0.285		
ADM 1,300 and above			0.127	0.145	0.145		
New Mexico			0.058	0.046	0.047	0.045	

The tendency for high-wealth districts to have relatively low tax rates (a negative elasticity) has lessened in California's high school and unified districts and in all three types of Kansas districts.

Income Neutrality

The school finance reform movement originally grew out of a concern for the distribution of revenues among districts serving students of various income levels. The association between districts' revenues per pupil and the average income of the populations they serve approximates this concept of fiscal neutrality. Table 9–4 presents the elasticities of revenues per pupil, instructional expenditures per pupil, and adjusted tax rates with respect to household income per pupil.

Table 9–4. Elasticity of Revenues per Pupil and Instructional Expenditures per Pupil with Respect to Household Income per Pupil.

State and Variable	Prereform			Postreform			
	1970–71	1971–72	1972–73	1973–74	1974–75	1975–76	1976–77
Revenues							
California							
Elementary	0.197	0.199	0.198	0.197	0.185	0.160	0.149
High school	0.268	0.274	0.255	0.262	0.219	0.184	0.134
Unified	0.210	0.185	0.099	0.151	0.101	0.106	0.093
Florida			0.087			0.306	
Kansas							
ADM below 400			0.176	0.204	0.240		
ADM 400 1,299			0.227	0.275	0.375		
ADM 1,300 and above			0.201	0.240	0.231		
Michigan		0.274	0.252	0.251	0.233	0.150	
New Mexico			0.044	0.017	0.001	0.000	
Instructional expenditures							
California							
Elementary	0.145	0.146	0.152	0.135	0.136	0.126	0.124
High school	0.153	0.150	0.153	0.116	0.099	0.072	0.077
Unified	0.183	0.204	0.182	0.131	0.135	0.118	0.110
Florida			0.099			0.348	
Kansas							
ADM below 400			0.159	0.232	0.226		
ADM 400 to 1,299			0.273	0.331	0.326		
ADM 1,300 and above			0.291	0.264	0.233		
New Mexico			0.180	0.177	0.198	0.209	

By this measure, reform improved the income neutrality of per-pupil revenues in Michigan and California, particularly in the latter's high school and unified districts, and worsened it in all three types of Kansas districts. Florida's reform introduced substantial income bias into what had been an income-neutral distribution of revenues. New Mexico's district revenues were independent of income both before and after reform.

Reform improved the income neutrality of the distributions of instructional expenditures in California's high school and unified districts, but introduced more income bias in Florida, in Kansas's small districts, and possibly in New Mexico.

Among Kansas's small and medium-sized districts, the higher income districts tended to levy lower tax rates before reform (a negative elasticity of adjusted tax rates with respect to income). Reform reversed that relationship. Reform seems not to have affected the relationship between adjusted tax rates and income in Kansas's large districts or in the other states.

Only California's unified districts and New Mexico's districts possessed an income-neutral distribution of revenues after reform—and New Mexico had possessed one before reform. Among the postreform distributions of instructional expenditures, only California high school districts exhibit income neutrality. In three cases—Florida, and Kansas's small and medium-sized districts—reform introduced more income bias into the distribution of revenues. Aside from the improvements registered in California's high school and unified districts, reform has generally worsened fiscal neutrality defined in terms of the relationship between revenues, or instructional expenditures, and household income.

Effort Neutrality

A third version of the fiscal neutrality concept holds that equity is not violated if districts with high per-pupil revenues or expenditures obtained them because they shouldered heavier tax burdens. To the extent that variations in revenues or expenditures are explained by variations in adjusted tax rates, equal efforts are bringing forth equal returns. An increase in the elasticity of per-pupil revenues with respect to the tax rates implies that a given change in the tax rate will lead to a greater increase in tax revenues. Table 9–5 presents elasticities of per-pupil revenues and instructional expenditures with respect to effort measured by property tax rates.

Among California's high school and unified districts and in Kansas's small and medium-sized districts, higher taxing districts had lower revenues before reform (the elasticity of revenues with respect to the tax rate was negative). Reform revised the relationship, a clear improvement in effort neutrality. Effort fiscal neutrality of the revenue distribution was also improved in Kansas's large districts and in Michigan with reform. New Mexico, by eliminating all variation in local effort, reduced effort neutrality to zero. And Florida substantially lessened the relationship between districts' efforts and their rewards.

Kansas improved effort neutrality with regard to instructional expenditures. Elsewhere, such neutrality either was not affected (California's high school and unified districts) or substantially worsened (California's elementary districts, Florida, and New Mexico).

Table 9–5. Elasticity of Revenues per Pupil and Instructional Expenditures per Pupil with Respect to Adjusted Tax Rates.

State and Variable	Prereform			Postreform			
	1970–71	1971–72	1972–73	1973–74	1974–75	1975–76	1976–77
Revenues							
California							
Elementary	0.167	0.138	0.135	0.434	0.385	0.159	0.138
High school	−0.222	−0.284	−0.275	0.494	0.341	0.232	0.107
Unified	−0.186	−0.207	−0.351	0.216	0.152	0.039	0.037
Florida			0.581			0.145	
Kansas							
ADM below 400			0.097	0.549	0.145		
ADM 400 to 1,299			0.209	0.420	0.168		
ADM 1,300 and above			0.141	0.322	0.353		
Michigan		0.451	0.498	0.574	0.636	0.667	
New Mexico			0.306	−0.217	0.201	0.000	
Instructional expenditures							
California							
Elementary	0.259	0.235	0.257	0.422	0.300	0.073	0.029
High school	−0.057	−0.048	−0.097	0.225	0.070	−0.047	−0.103
Unified	−0.045	−0.056	−0.113	0.240	0.126	−0.007	−0.003
Florida			0.467			0.084	
Kansas							
ADM below 400			−0.125	0.491	0.093		
ADM 400 to 1,299			−0.201	0.376	0.204		
ADM 1,300 and above			0.223	0.242	0.317		
New Mexico			0.187	−0.143	0.014	0.000	

WINNERS AND LOSERS

What kinds of districts and students gained from reform? Who lost? To answer these questions, we ranked the students in each state according to the size of the district they attended. We then calculated the average revenues per pupil for students above and below the median. Table 9–6 presents the ratios of these two means, and similar ratios computed for districts above and below the median percentage urban, percentage white, and percentage populated by families whose income is below the poverty line. Tables 9–7 and 9–8 present similar ratios for the distibutions of instructional expenditures per pupil and of adjusted tax rates per pupil.

In any case, a ratio greater than one implies that students attending

Table 9–6. Ratios of Average Per-Pupil Revenues in Districts below the Median on a District Characteristic to Average Per-Pupil Revenues in Districts above the Median on the Characteristic.

State and Characteristic	Preform			Postreform			
	1970–71	1971–72	1972–73	1973–74	1974–75	1975–76	1976–77
Size							
California							
Elementary	1.04	1.05	1.06	1.04	1.08	1.07	1.05
High school	1.05	1.05	1.10	1.11	1.02	1.07	1.07
Unified	1.00	0.98	0.92	1.00	0.98	0.98	1.00
Florida			0.97			0.89	
Kansas							
ADM below 400			1.32	1.23	1.30		
ADM 400 to 1,299			1.16	1.13	1.12		
ADM 1,300 and above			0.96	0.91	0.93		
Michigan		0.90	0.93	0.90	0.91	0.91	
New Mexico			1.09	1.12	1.06	1.05	
% Urban							
California							
Elementary	0.93	0.93	0.93	0.94	0.96	0.95	0.96
High school	0.96	0.97	0.99	1.00	0.98	1.02	1.02
Unified	0.95	0.93	0.89	0.96	0.95	0.95	0.97
Florida			0.96			0.88	
Kansas							
ADM below 400			1.10	1.09	0.99		
ADM 400 to 1,299			1.11	1.04	1.11		
ADM 1,300 and above			0.95	0.90	0.94		
Michigan		0.90	0.93	0.88	0.88	0.88	
New Mexico			1.09	1.10	1.04	1.01	
% White							
California							
Elementary	1.01	1.01	1.02	1.02	1.00	1.01	1.02
High school	1.07	1.06	1.05	1.07	1.05	1.05	1.06
Unified	1.05	1.06	1.14	1.04	1.06	1.05	1.04
Florida			1.06			1.05	
Kansas							
ADM below 400			0.84	0.91	0.99		
ADM 400 to 1,299			0.90	0.93	0.94		
ADM 1,300 and above			0.98	1.03	0.99		
Michigan		1.04	1.00	1.04	1.03	1.03	
New Mexico			1.08	1.06	0.99	0.98	
% Poverty							
California							
Elementary	1.15	1.16	1.15	1.10	1.10	1.08	1.08
High school	1.10	1.09	1.09	1.07	1.07	1.03	1.02
Unified	0.99	0.97	0.93	1.00	0.97	0.98	0.98
Florida			1.06			1.18	
Kansas							
ADM below 400			0.97	1.08	1.20		
ADM 400 to 1,299			1.00	0.99	1.01		
ADM 1,300 and above			1.06	1.08	1.07		
Michigan		1.06	1.10	1.05	1.06	1.06	
New Mexico			0.98	0.99	1.00	1.01	

Table 9–7. Ratios of Average Per-Pupil Instructional Expenditures in Districts below the Median on a District Characteristic to Average Per-Pupil Instructional Expenditures in Districts above the Median on the Characteristic.

State and Characteristic	Prereform			Postreform			
	1970–71	1971–72	1972–73	1973—74	1974–75	1975–76	1976–77
Size							
California							
Elementary	0.98	0.99	0.98	0.96	1.02	1.01	1.01
High school	1.02	1.02	1.05	1.07	1.02	1.05	1.02
Unified	0.96	0.97	0.95	0.94	0.98	1.01	0.99
Florida			0.96			0.89	
Kansas							
ADM below 400			1.25	1.21	1.21		
ADM 400 to 1,299			1.12	1.12	1.14		
ADM 1,300 and above			0.90	0.93	0.94		
New Mexico			1.07	1.06	1.04	1.07	
% Urban							
California							
Elementary	0.93	0.91	0.91	0.92	0.96	0.95	0.94
High school	0.99	0.99	0.99	1.02	1.05	1.05	1.05
Unified	0.96	0.98	0.96	0.95	0.98	1.01	1.03
Florida			0.96			0.85	
Kansas							
ADM below 400							
ADM 400 to 1,299			1.07	1.05	1.05		
ADM 1,300 and above			0.89	0.93	0.94		
New Mexico			1.02	1.02	0.99	0.97	
% White							
California							
Elementary	1.04	1.04	1.04	1.05	1.02	1.02	0.99
High school	1.08	1.06	1.06	1.06	1.06	1.10	1.09
Unified	1.08	1.08	1.10	1.10	1.04	1.01	0.99
Florida			1.06			1.10	
Kansas							
ADM below 400			0.91	0.91	0.94		
ADM 400 to 1,299			0.92	0.93	0.92		
ADM 1,300 and above			1.01	0.98	0.97		
New Mexico			1.00	1.00	0.98	0.97	
% Poverty							
California							
Elementary	1.09	1.10	1.11	1.07	1.11	1.12	1.13
High school	1.05	1.05	1.06	1.03	1.02	1.00	0.99
Unified	0.96	0.97	0.95	0.94	0.98	1.00	1.03
Florida			1.06			1.18	
Kansas							
ADM below 400			1.05	1.09	1.11		
ADM 400 to 1,299			1.01	1.00	1.01		
ADM 1,300 and above			1.09	1.07	1.06		
New Mexico			1.01	1.00	1.04	1.04	

Table 9–8. Ratios of Average Adjusted Tax Rates in Districts below the Median on a District Characteristic to Average Adjusted Tax Rates in Districts above the Median on the Characteristic.

State and Characteristic	Prereform			Postreform			
	1970–71	1971–72	1972–73	1973—74	1974–75	1975–76	1976–77
Size							
California							
Elementary	0.86	0.85	0.84	0.89	0.93	0.91	0.90
High school	0.91	0.90	0.88	0.99	0.95	0.98	0.97
Unified	1.00	0.98	1.00	0.97	0.93	0.96	0.96
Florida			0.93			0.96	
Kansas							
ADM below 400			0.95	1.17	0.99		
ADM 400 to 1,299			0.93	0.93	0.97		
ADM 1,300 and above			0.78	0.73	0.80		
Michigan		0.88	0.92	0.87	0.88	0.88	
New Mexico			1.07	1.16	0.97	1.00	
% Urban							
California							
Elementary	0.88	0.89	0.90	0.90	0.93	0.95	0.95
High school	0.98	0.97	1.00	0.99	1.00	1.06	1.01
Unified	1.04	1.02	1.05	1.00	0.93	0.98	0.97
Florida			0.95			0.99	
Kansas							
ADM below 400			1.00	1.04	0.95		
ADM 400 to 1,299			0.89	0.96	0.94		
ADM 1,300 and above			0.75	0.72	0.80		
Michigan		0.89	0.93	0.86	0.86	0.87	
New Mexico			1.03	1.08	0.97	1.00	
% White							
California							
Elementary	1.01	1.02	1.02	1.02	1.02	1.04	1.06
High school	0.94	0.92	0.91	0.95	0.96	0.98	1.01
Unified	0.99	0.99	0.98	1.02	1.07	1.02	1.04
Florida			1.05			1.05	
Kansas							
ADM below 400			1.12	0.96	1.03		
ADM 400 to 1,299			1.11	1.03	1.07		
ADM 1,300 and above			1.16	1.18	1.11		
Michigan		0.99	0.93	1.01	1.02	1.01	
New Mexico			1.17	1.18	1.04	1.00	
% Poverty							
California							
Elementary	1.17	1.17	1.16	1.17	1.10	1.07	1.05
High school	1.09	1.06	1.06	1.09	1.06	1.00	0.98
Unified	1.07	1.07	1.09	1.04	0.97	1.01	0.99
Florida			0.97			0.99	
Kansas							
ADM below 400			0.90	1.05	1.08		
ADM 400 to 1,299			1.05	1.07	1.02		
ADM 1,300 and above			1.24	1.20	1.12		
Michigan		1.18	1.26	1.14	1.11	1.11	
New Mexico			0.99	0.98	1.05	1.00	

districts below the median on the relevant characteristic averaged greater amounts of the variable in question than did students attending districts above the median. Ratios less then one imply the converse.

The ratios in Tables 9–6 through 9–8 suggest that:

- Reform has generally not affected the distributions of per-pupil revenues or of instructional expenditures, among different kinds of districts.
- Reform has not affected disparities in adjusted tax rates among large and small, more and less urban, and more and less minority districts.
- Reform has substantially reduced disparities in adjusted tax rates between more and less poverty-prone districts.

There are a few exceptions to the first conclusion. Florida's reform, for example, has channeled relatively greater revenues per pupil to its larger, its more urban, and its less poverty-prone districts. Kansas's reform has shifted per-pupil revenues toward the more urban, the less white, and the less poverty-prone of its small districts. And reform in New Mexico has shifted per-pupil revenues toward the state's more urban and more white districts. But these are exceptions, in that we find the ratio of per pupil revenues in small districts (compared to relatively large districts) largely unaffected by reform. Similarly, reform has not much affected the division of revenues between less and more urban districts, between less and more white districts, and between districts where the incidence of poverty is low and those where it is high.

Even fewer exceptions occur with instructional expenditures. In Florida, reform has led to a relative decline in the per-pupil instructional expenditures of smaller, of less urban, and of more poverty-prone districts; and among Kansas's small districts, the less poverty-prone enjoyed a relative gain. None of the remaining cases show changes that exceed 5 percentage points after reform.

The one set of results that reveal substantial effects of reform pertain to the distribution of adjusted tax rates between low-poverty and high-poverty districts. Before reform, adjusted tax rates in all three types of California's districts, in Kansas's medium-sized and large districts, and in Michigan, were substantially higher in low-poverty districts. In every case, reform was accompanied by relative reductions in tax burdens; in four cases—California's elementary and unified districts, Kansas's large districts, and Michigan—the reductions were large. Among Kansas's small districts, the less poverty-prone enjoyed low tax rates before reform but found themselves facing high ones afterward.

Elsewhere, the only departures from the general pattern of little change occurred in New Mexico (which fully equalized tax rates), Kansas's small districts (where reform largely eliminated the advantage of white districts), and California's unified districts (where reform shifted the advantage from more urban to less urban districts).

CONCLUSIONS

The original proponents of school finance reform viewed it as an issue of educational equity. They assumed that greater school spending is associated with better schooling, therefore that disparities in one imply disparities in the other. They also assumed that poor people live in property-poor districts, at least more so than in property-rich districts. Finally, they observed that state finance systems were only mildly equalizing at best, and argued that those systems discriminate against poor children by affording them an education inferior to that of better-off children.

These arguments were supported by the *Serrano* decision, whereupon efforts to revise state school finance systems soon spread across the nation. The issue has aroused extensive public debate in most states, and has spurred legislative or judicial action in many. At least twenty-five states have substantially modified their systems in response to reform pressures.

It would be rash to equate change with reform, however. Judging by the experiences of the five states reviewed here, the reform movement's victories are somewhat hollow. These states have made some progress toward a more equal distribution of revenues per pupil, but most of the improvements have been small, and in many cases there has been no improvement at all. The record appears even more bleak if, as seems likely, instructional expenditures per pupil are more closely linked to educational quality than are revenues per pupil. Reform has done nothing at all to equalize the distribution of per-pupil instructional expenditures.

How have poor children—or, more accurately, districts serving disproportionate numbers of poor children—fared in comparsion with their more prosperous counterparts? Not well! California's reform went part of the way toward reducing the associations between a district's revenues and instructional expenditures, on the one hand, and the average income of its population, on the other hand—but those variables still remain significantly associated with household income. Florida and Kansas slipped backward: Their reforms introduced significant income bias into what had been income-neutral distributions of per-pupil revenues and instructional expenditures. Similarly, the distributions of instructional expenditures generally shifted in favor of districts in which the incidence of poverty was below the median, and away from the poorest districts. If anything, reform has worked in favor of people who were already better off.

Reform has brought only feeble improvement in either ex ante fiscal neutrality or wealth neutrality. California districts' revenues are now somewhat more closely related to their efforts and less so to their wealth, but progress in either respect has been far from impressive. And elsewhere, reform has failed to achieve distributions of revenues or instructional expenditures that reflect fiscal efforts more or reflect wealth less.

All in all, reforms in these five states have not greatly reduced the problems that inspired the reform movement. There are some bright spots—some improvements in educational equity—but after the flurry of changes had settled down, reform turned out to be much ado about nothing, for the most part. Overall, each state's prereform and postreform distributions of expenditures remain a close match. Educational equity is still a distant goal.

These reforms have made considerable progress toward other objectives, however—notably, toward tax equity. In every case except Florida, disparities in adjusted tax rates have narrowed dramatically. And reform brought greater equity to the distributions of adjusted tax rates between large and small districts, between more and less urban districts, between districts serving few whites and many, and between more and less poverty-prone districts. Reform seems to have been an effective device for equalizing the burdens of supporting education.

It also appears that reform has promoted the objective of increasing statewide spending for education. In principle, equalization could have taken the form of redistributing revenues from high-spending to low-spending districts—but realistic politicians are disinclined to play Robin Hood in that way. Instead, reform states have chosen the more expensive alternative of increasing the total amount of educational aid, attempting thereby to raise lower spending districts' revenues while leaving those of higher spending districts pretty much as they were. California, for example, increased state contributions per pupil to districts' general funds by 48 percent, and the first year of reform in Kansas saw a 44-percent increase in state general fund support per pupil. Reform-year increases in state general aid per pupil were less dramatic in Michigan and New Mexico, 11 and 14 percent, respectively; nonetheless, they represent substantial increases in the costs of education to those states. (We lack data on Florida's general aid to education in its first reform year.) To be sure, the states might have increased their educational spending somewhat even without reform. The major point here, however, is that legislators thus far have taken the costlier route toward equity: wholesale increases in the state budget for education. They have done so because of their reluctance to tax high-spending districts to support education in lower spending districts, although it would be cheaper to achieve equity in that way.

WHY REFORM DID NOT ACHIEVE MORE

The rhetoric of school finance reform has focused on disparities in school district spending. Virtually all participants in the reform debate—the courts, state legislators and executives, the press, and numerous private individuals and agencies—have framed their remarks in the context of revenue (or spending) equalization or fiscal neutrality. The reform laws enacted thus far, according to their preambles and the speeches and press releases that accompanied them, were designed to bring about more equal or fiscally neutral distributions of revenues.

By those criteria, reform has not accomplished a great deal. There has been some progress toward equalization and fiscal neutrality, but one is led to wonder why the complete restructuring of state school finance systems has fallen short of its ostensible goals. Below, we offer some possible explanations.

Diverse Objectives

Each of the reforms appears to have been designed to serve a motley assortment of purposes simultaneously. We do not mean to imply that the plans' developers, or the legislators who enacted them, or the governors who signed them into law, necessarily had any particular set of objectives in mind. But regardless of what they wanted to accomplish, or thought that the plans would accomplish, the structures of the plans are compromises among diverse, and sometimes conflicting, goals.

We have noted the tension between equalization and fiscal neutrality. Although much of the school finance literature describes these concerns as alternative paths converging on the same goal of equity, they are in fact two separate paths leading to two separate goals based on differing concepts of equity. It is unlikely that all the districts in a state would choose to levy the same tax rate under any school finance system, even if doing so would yield the same revenues per pupil for all of them. The only way to achieve a high degree of equalization, consequently, is to impose narrow constraints on school districts' freedom of decision regarding budgets and tax rates, which means a loss of local control—but local control is central to the concept of fiscal neutrality.

A school finance plan can be oriented toward fiscal neutrality, as is Michigan's, or toward equalization, as is New Mexico's. Or it can compromise. California, Florida, and Kansas enacted compromise plans in the sense that, unlike New Mexico, they permit districts to determine their own tax rates and, hence, revenues; but, unlike Michigan, they limit districts' choices. The limits hinder progress toward fiscal neutrality, while the permitted discretion impairs equalization.

We are not suggesting that such compromises are in any sense "wrong" or "improper." Rather, we are suggesting that local control over budgets and tax rates is the "price" of equalization, and that revenue and tax rate disparities are the "price" of fiscal neutrality. More generally, equalization entails the sacrifice of local discretion over spending and tax levels; one reason that these plans have not provided greater equity is their attempt to preserve some degree of local discretion.

These plans also reflect the three-way conflict among "holding harmless" high-spending districts, tax relief, and state support for education. None of the reform plans we studied cut the revenues of previously high-spending districts. In fact, none even capped spending. Their various revenue limits and tax-rate limits only constrained the growth of revenues in high-spending districts. Consequently, the distance that previously low-spending districts had to travel to catch up to their higher spending counterparts increased each year. The states increased their aid to low-spending districts, but the limits that held down revenue growth in the high-spending districts also applied, though not always as tightly, to low-spending districts, which had to translate some of their increased state aid into tax relief.

Political realities may impose a "leveling-up" equalization strategy, but that approach is expensive; and the amount of equalization accomplished at a given cost to the state diminishes as state funds are translated into tax relief.

It is not within our province to judge whether equalization is more important than tax relief, or whether the revenues of high-spending districts should be cut to improve equalization, or whether states should contribute more to the support of education. We merely point out that leveling up is done at the cost of either greater state support for education or higher local property taxes, or both. States can obtain greater equality at a given level of support only by redirecting revenues from high-spending to low-spending districts or allowing lower spending districts to increase their tax rates. They can provide more tax relief or greater equality of tax burdens only by redirecting revenues from high-spending to low-spending districts or by increasing state aid to education. The five states' reforms generally eased local property tax rates and very substantially equalized tax efforts across districts. The price of these results was retarded progress toward revenue equalization, given the states' ability or willingness to support education and their inability or unwillingness to cut the revenues of high-spending districts.

Add-Ons and Adjustments[3]

Each of the reform plans can be viewed as a combination of a basic plan and various add-ons and adjustments that modify the distribution of state aid among districts. California adds a flat-grant program ($125 per pupil) to its foundation program and permits districts to override their revenue limits with approval of the voters. Florida adjusts the distribution of state aid according to the distribution of pupils among twenty-six categories in each district and to the cost of living in the district. Kansas rebates a share of the state personal income tax receipts

---

[3]The add-ons and adjustments discussed here are those in operation in each state in the years covered by our data. Some of the states have recently added, deleted, or modified such provisions, but we lack the data to assess the consequences.

collected in each county to the county's school districts. Michigan's municipal overburden provision provides additional state aid to cities where nonschool tax burdens are particularly high. And New Mexico adjusts state aid according to the distribution of districts' pupils among grades and to an index of teacher costs.

These provisions have been justified on several different grounds: California's flat-grant program is constitutionally mandated; its override provision presumably allows districts that are willing to exert greater tax effort for the schools an opportunity to do so. Florida's, Michigan's, and New Mexico's provisions ostensibly direct additional state aid to districts judged to have needs that are not well accommodated by the basic plan. And the income tax rebate in Kansas is supposedly a means for shifting part of the school support burden to the income tax.

Some subtle parliamentary maneuvering apparently has gone on behind the scene as well, however. Persons familiar with state school finance systems have told us, off the record, of instances where states have included add-ons or adjustments to "hold harmless" high-spending districts. Allegedly, states that were under political or judicial pressure to reform, but unable either to cut the revenues of high-spending districts or provide enough additional state aid to level-up low-spending districts, found an ingenious way out. They searched for a characteristic that was common to high-spending districts and rare in low-spending districts. They then provided an aid adjustment to "offset the unusual costs" incurred by districts with that characteristic. The result was an obstensibly equitable school finance plan that preserved the revenues of high-spending districts but did not require additional state support to the others.

In any event, whatever the purposes of add-ons or adjustments might have been, and however appropriate they might be to the circumstances of a particular state, their effects on equalization and fiscal neutrality are of interest.

California's flat grants are counted against a district's foundation aid, and therefore add nothing to the revenues of districts receiving foundation support. Nearly half the districts in the state, however, are not entitled to foundation support because their tax bases are so large;[4] but these districts receive the flat grants, which thereby partially offset the equalizing effects of the foundation program.

---

[4]A district is not entitled to foundation support if its property tax base is so large that its (hypothetical) local revenues at the computational tax rate exceed the foundation guarantee.

The ability to override the revenue limit (formally, to levy a tax rate in excess of the rate that yields the revenue limit) reduced the equalization effect of the revenue limits. More important, high-wealth and high-spending districts most frequently obtained overrides. Thus, both equalization and fiscal neutrality were impaired by the override provision.

Florida's pupil-weighting system has no impact whatsoever on the distribution of revenues. The correlation between weighted pupils and unweighted pupils across Florida's districts is extremely high (greater than 0.999). A foundation plan that guaranteed about 1.26 times as much support per unweighted pupil would have led to exactly the same distribution of revenues. The cost-of-living adjustment, however, has a decided effect on the distribution of revenues; it introduces substantial revenue disparities. Moreover, the cost of living tends to be high where wealth, and particularly income, are high. The adjustment therefore directs additional revenues to high-wealth and high-income districts, adversely affecting wealth neutrality and introducing very substantial income bias into the distribution of revenues.

Kansas's income tax rebate essentially provides support in proportion to the taxable income of a county's residents. School districts in high-income counties therefore levy lower property tax rates to stay within their budget limit. The net effect is a reduction in the property taxes paid by residents of higher income counties.

Michigan's municipal overburden provision distributes a small amount of funds, most of which go to Detroit. Because Detroit has above-average per-pupil revenues and wealth, the provision is disequalizing and reduces fiscal neutrality. However, the amount of funds involved is so small relative to state equalization aid that the adverse effects on equalization and fiscal neutrality are negligible.

The teachers' cost-adjustment provision in New Mexico's reform plan allows greater revenues to districts whose teachers are relatively highly educated and experienced. We suspect that this provision accounts for the rather surprising New Mexico results. The state shifted from the least-equalizing prereform finance system—flat grants—to a plan tantamount to full state assumption. Yet this shift accounted for a reduction of only about 20 percent in revenue disparities. The puzzling question is why a shift from a flat-grant system to a system that ostensibly guaranteed equal revenues to every district failed to bring about greater equaltiy. The reason, we suspect, is that some of New Mexico's districts took advantage of their opportunities prior to reform and raised greater per-pupil revenues than did other districts.

They then used these funds to employ more educated and experienced teachers than lower wealth districts could afford. Their teachers' experience and education index accordingly would be relatively high in postreform years, raising their revenue entitlements according to the formula.

We could not explicitly test this hypothesis, because the data we obtained did not provide information on teachers' experience and education adjustment factors. However, it is consistent with available data. Note also that this feature of New Mexico's plan has a tendency to lock in revenue disparities whether or not they are associated with wealth. A district that entered the reform era with a highly educated and experienced staff had a high adjustment factor, generating high revenues that allowed it to retain a highly qualified staff. In contrast, a district with a much less qualified staff at the outset of reform had a low adjustment factor, generating lower revenues, and therefore could not as readily hire highly qualified new teachers. This feature of the plan consequently appears to run counter to the ultimate objective of reform: reducing interdistrict disparities in the quality of education offered to children.

The fiscal limits or constraints imposed by California, Florida, Kansas, and New Mexico have also figured importantly in their reforms. Depending on one's point of view, revenue or tax rate limits may be interpreted as devices for bringing about gradual equalization, for delaying equalization, for limiting disparities in a system that permits local discretion, for controlling the cost of state aid, or for forcing local districts to translate a part of their state aid into local property tax relief.

Reform as a Preventive to Further Disparity

Our study compared prereform and postreform distributions and relationships in five states. Most states annually reset their school finance systems' parameters, and year-to-year increases in state aid to education are common. It is beyond the scope of this study to speculate on what changes the five states would have made if they had not restructured their finance systems, and how those changes would have affected the distributions and relationships of interest. But it is possible, perhaps even likely, that disparities in these states would have widened in the absence of reform. If so, these reforms have been more successful than suggested by the data examined here.

REFERENCES

Alexander, Arthur. 1974. *Teachers, Salaries, and School District Expenditures*. R-1588-FF. Santa Monica, Calif.: The Rand Corporation.

Averch, Harvey; Stephen J. Carroll; Theodore S. Donaldson; Herbert J. Kiesling; and John Pincus. 1974. *How Effective Is Schooling? A Critical Review of Research*. Englewood Cliffs, N. J.: Educational Technology Publications.

Barro, Stephen. 1974. "Alternative Post-Serrano Systems and Their Implications." In J. Pincus (ed.), *School Finance in Transition*, pp. 25–80. Cambridge, Mass.: Ballinger Publishing Company.

Barro, Stephen, and Stephen J. Carroll. 1975. *Budget Allocation by School Districts: An Analysis of Spending for Teachers and Other Resources*. R-1797-NIE. Santa Monica, Calif.: The Rand Corporation.

Berne, Robert. 1978. *Methodological Assessment of Education Equity and Wealth Neutrality Measures*. New York: Public Policy Research Institute, New York University.

Brown, Lawrence; Alan L. Ginsburg; J. Neil Killalea; Richard A. Rosthal; and Esther O. Tron. 1977. *School Finance Reform in the Seventies, Achievements and Failures*. Technical Analysis Paper. Washington, D. C.: Office of the Assistant Secretary for Planning and Evaluation, Department of Health, Education, and Welfare, and Killalea Associates, Inc.

Carroll, Stephen J. 1976. "School District Expenditure Behavior." *Journal of Human Resources* 11 (Summer): 317–327.

Carroll, Stephen J. 1979. *The Search for Equity in School Finance: Results from Five States*. R-2348-NIE. Santa Monica, Calif.: The Rand Corporation.

175

Coons, John; William Clune III; and Stephen Sugarman. 1970. *Private Wealth and Public Education.* Cambridge, Mass.: Harvard University Press.

Feldstein, Martin. 1975. "Wealth Neutrality and Local Choice in Public Education." *American Economic Review* 65 (March): 75–89.

Ladd, Helen F. 1975. "Local Education Expenditures, Fiscal Capacity, and the Composition of the Property Tax Base." *National Tax Journal* 28 (June): 145–158.

National Educational Finance Project. 1971. *Status and Impact of Educational Finance Programs.* Gainesville, Fla.

Park, Rolla Edward, and Stephen J. Carroll. 1982. *Michigan School District Response to a Guaranteed Tax Base: A Time-Series Cross-Section Analysis.* N-1599-DHEW. Santa Monica, Calif.: The Rand Corporation.

Park, Rolla Edward, and Stephen J. Carroll. 1979. *The Search for Equity in School Finance: Michigan School District Response to a Guaranteed Tax Base.* R-2393-NIE/HEW. Santa Monica, Calif.: The Rand Corporation.

U. S. Office of Education. 1972. *Public School Finance Programs, 1971-72.* Publication No. (OE) 73-00001. Washington, D.C.: Department of Health, Education, and Welfare.

Wise, Arthur. 1968. *Rich Schools, Poor Schools.* Chicago: University of Chicago Press.

RAND EDUCATIONAL POLICY STUDIES

PUBLISHED

Averch, Harvey A.; Stephen J. Carroll; Theodore S. Donaldson; Herbert J. Kiesling; and John Pincus. *How Effective Is Schooling? A Critical Review of Research.* Englewood Cliffs, N.J.: Educational Technology Publications, 1974.

Carpenter-Huffman, P.; G.R. Hall; and G.C. Sumner. *Change in Education: Insights from Performance Contracting.* Cambridge, Mass.: Ballinger Publishing Company, 1974.

Carroll, Stephen J., and Rolla E. Park. *The Search for Equity in School Finance.* Cambridge, Mass.: Ballinger Publishing Company, 1982.

Crain, Robert L.; Rita E. Manhard; and Ruth E. Narot. *Making Desegregation Work: How Schools Create Social Climates.* Cambridge, Mass.: Ballinger Publishing Company, 1982.

Elmore, Richard, and Milbrey W. McLaughlin. *Reform and Retrenchment: The Politics of California School Finance Reform.* Cambridge, Mass.: Ballinger Publishing Company, 1982.

Gurwitz, Aaron S. *The Economics of Public School Finance.* Cambridge, Mass.: Ballinger Publishing Company, 1982.

McLaughlin, Milbrey W. *Evaluation and Reform: The Elementary and Secondary Education Act of 1965. Title I.* Cambridge, Mass.: Ballinger Publishing Company, 1975.

Pincus, John, ed. *School Finance in Transition: The Courts and Educational Reform.* Cambridge, Mass.: Ballinger Publishing Company, 1974.

Timpane, Michael, ed. *The Federal Interest in Financing Schooling.* Cambridge, Mass.: Ballinger Publishing Company, 1978

OTHER RAND BOOKS IN EDUCATION

Burno, James E., ed. *Emerging Issues in Education: Policy Implications for the Schools.* Lexington, Mass.: D. C. Heath and Co., 1972.

Coleman, James S., and Nancy L. Karweit. *Information Systems and Performance Measures in Schools.* Englewood Cliffs, N.J.: Educational Technology Publications, 1972.

Haggart, Sue A., ed. *Program Budgeting for School District Planning.* Englewood Cliffs, N.J.: Educational Technology Publications, 1972.

Levien, Roger E. *The Emerging Technology: Instructional Uses of the Computer in Higher Education.* New York: McGraw-Hill Book Co., 1972.

INDEX

Alamagordo (NM), 137
Albuquerque (NM), 137
Alternative programs, 125
Annual Report of the Commissioner of Education, 81
Annual Statistical Report, 97
Atomic Energy Commission funds, 137
Average daily attendance (ADA)
  in California, 41–42, 43, 44–45
  in Florida, 81
  in Michigan, 123
Average daily membership (ADM)
  in Kansas, 97
  in New Mexico, 135–137

Board of Tax Appeals, 93
Books, 80, 135, 136
Bureau of School Apportionments, 46

California (*see also* specific subject)
  adjusted tax rates, 61
  effects of reform, 11–12, 41–77
  postreform system, 42–43
  prereform system, 41–42
  reform in, 2–3

reform plans, 9–10, 11
Senate Bill, 90, 20
state aid in, 77
summary data, 44–45, 46–57
years of data, 6
California State Assessor's Office, 46
California State Department of Education, 46
California Supreme Court, 2, 3, 34
Capital stocks, disparities in, 24–25
Categorical aid programs, 50, 101
  (*see also* Federal Aid; Public Law 874; State aid)
  equalization and, 25
Community action program funds, 127
Compensatory education, 125
County school tax levy, 137, 140

Dade County (FL), 90
Data sources, 38–39
  California, 46–47
  Florida, 81
  Kansas, 97
  Michigan, 125
  New Mexico, 139–140

179

Debt service equalization, 125
Derby (KS), 95
Detroit (MI), 173
Distributional equality, reform and,
    32–34, 155–157
District power equalizing (DPE)
    plans, 27, 28
    defined, 10n
District size
    in Florida, 88–90
    in Kansas, 120–121
    and reform, 72–73, 74–75, 131,
        132, 162–167
DPE (see District power equalizing
    plans)
Driver training, 43, 80, 95, 97, 98

Edson (KS), 94n
Educable retarded, 95
Effort neutrality, 161–162
Emergency school assistance, 127,
    139
Equality (see also specific subject)
    distributional, 155–157
    and fiscal neutrality, 27–29, 157–
        162
    historical background of reform,
        1–5
    measurement of, 21–23
    and school resources, 21–23
    taxes and, 1–2
Equalization aid program, 136, 139
Exceptional programs, 80, 95
Expenditure equality, 33n
Expenditure-oriented measure, 26
Expenditures (see Per pupil
    expenditures; Instructional
    expenditures)

Federal aid, 25 (see also Public
    Law 874)
    to California, 50–51
    to Michigan, 127, 129
    to New Mexico, 137
Federal impact aid (see Public Law
    874)

Federal regulation of funds, 30
Fiscal constraints, 20, 174
Fiscal neutrality, 5, 31, 157–162, 170
    in California, 52
    concept of, 27–29
    in Kansas, 121
    measures of, 34–37
    in Michigan, 131, 133
    in New Mexico, 15, 147, 148
Fiscal Transactions, 46
Flat grant distribution plan, 19,
    148, 171, 172, 173
Florida (see also specific subject)
    categorical programs, 83–85
    data sources, 81
    effects of reform in, 12–13, 79–91
    number of districts, 81
    pupil weights in, 22n, 82
    reform plans, 10, 11
    revenue sources, 81
    weighting in, 23
    years for data, 6
Florida Racing Commission Funds,
    80, 81, 83, 84
Forest Reserve funds, 137, 139
Fort Leavenworth (KS), 94n, 95, 96
Foundation plan, 23, 28–29, 171,
    172
    in California, 9, 41–42
    defined, 9n
    and equalization, 18n, 18–19
    in Florida, 10, 79, 80, 81–82, 173
    in Kansas, 13, 93, 94
    in Michigan, 123–124, 125

Gallup(NM), 137
Gifted minors, 43
Guaranteed tax base (GTB) plan
    defined, 10n
    in Kansas, 10, 12, 95, 119, 121
    in Michigan, 10, 133n

Handicapped, education for, 43, 124,
    136
Head Start, 127
High school districts, 12, 55, 58–66
Hutchinson (KS), 94n

Impact aid, 3 (*see also* Public Law 874)
  in Florida, 82
  in Kansas, 96, 97
  in Michigan, 127–128
  in New Mexico, 137
Income
  in Kansas, 111
  mean for, 36
  and per pupil revenues, 109
  regression on, 36
  and tax burdens, 27
Income equality, 27, 158, 159–161
Income neutrality, 159–161
  in California, 12, 52–55, 61–63,
    70–72, 76
  in Florida, 83–89
  in Kansas, 102–104, 109–111,
    117
  in Michigan, 14, 129–131
  in New Mexico, 143–144
  per pupil revenues and, 61–63
Income tax rebate, 96, 98, 108, 114,
    116, 121, 172, 173
Indian students, 137
Instructional expenditures, 30–31, 158–
    159, 162–167 (*see also* Per pupil
    expenditures)
  California, 52–53, 77, 152, 153, 154
  Florida, 83–85, 86, 88–90, 152, 154
  Kansas, 99–102, 107–109, 114–116,
    118–119, 120, 121, 152, 154
  Michigan, 152, 153
  New Mexico, 140–143, 147, 152,
    153
  summarized, 152
  wealth neutrality and, 61–63
Intercultural Development Research
    Association, 139

Johnson-O'Malley Act, 137
Junction (KS), 95

Kansas (*see also* specific subject)
  data sources, 97
  definition of wealth in, 28
  effects of reform in, 13–14, 93–121
  federal impact aid in, 25, 30

foundation plan, 93, 94
  postreform system, 95–97
  prereform system, 93–95
  reform plans, 10, 11, 119, 121
  tax neutrality, 117
  years for data, 6
Kansas State Department of Educa-
    tion, 97
K–12 districts, 125

Los Alamos Laboratory of AEC, 137

McDermott, John, 3
Massachusetts, 19n
Matching grant plans, 19
Mentally retarded, education of, 43,
    124
Michigan, 173 (*see also* specific
    subject)
  data sources, 125
  effects of reform in, 14, 123–133
  General Fund Revenue, 126
  prereform plans, 123–124
  reform plans, 10, 124–125
  summary information, 126, 127
  years for data, 6
Michigan State Department of
    Education, 125
Mineral lease income, 136
Minorities, 63–66, 88–90, 104–106,
    112–114, 118–119, 145, 147
Moscow (KS), 94n
Motor vehicle license fees, 137, 139
Mullenville (KS), 94n
Municipal overburden aid, 125, 173

National Conference of State
    Legislatures, 81, 97
National Educational Finance Project,
    18n, 19n
New Mexico (*see also* specific subject)
  data sources, 139–140
  effects of reform in, 15, 135–149
  federal impact aid in, 25, 30
  House Bill 85, 138
  prereform plans, 135, 145, 147–148
  reform plans, 10–11, 138–139, 147–149

revenue sources, 139–140
Senate Bill 9, 139
teachers' cost-adjustment provision,
    173–174
years for data, 6
New York, 19n

Percentiles, 33
Per pupil expenditures, 100, 101–102
California, 51–52, 55–59, 60, 69,
    70, 72–77
distributional equality measures,
    32–34
distribution of, 156–157
instructional, 30–31, 61–63
New Mexico, 147
wealth neutrality and, 62–63
Per pupil revenues
California, 50–52, 54–55, 56–59,
    60, 72–77
defined, 11n
distributional equality measures,
    32–34
and fiscal neutrality, 52
Florida, 83–85
general, 29–30, 66–70
general plus PL 874, 30, 67–70
Kansas, 99–102, 106–109, 112–116,
    117–119
local plus state, 67–70
local plus state plus PL 874, 30
measures of, 29–31
Michigan, 127, 131
New Mexico, 140–149
nonfederal, 30
reform and, 70–72, 151–154
total, 30, 67–70
wealth neutrality and, 61–63
Poverty prone districts
Florida, 88–90
Kansas, 104–106, 112–114,
    120, 121
Michigan, 131, 133
New Mexico, 145–147
reform and, 63–66, 73, 74–75
Property, tax exempt, 30
Property taxes, 27
California, 3, 46, 61

Kansas, 99
Michigan, 127
New Mexico, 144
Proposition 13, 3
Public Law 874, 3, 25, 30, 50, 51,
    67, 82, 83, 99, 100, 101
in Florida, 82
in Kansas, 92, 108, 116
in Michigan, 127, 139
in New Mexico, 15, 137, 140–143,
    145, 146–148
Public Law 89–10, 30
Pupil weighting
defined, 22–23, 22n
in Florida, 82
in New Mexico, 138, 142

Race (see Minorities)
Reading support program, 125
Reform
add-ons and adjustments, 171–174
background of, 17–19, 167
defined, 2n
determining effects of, 37–38
and distributional equality, 155–157
effects summarized, 15–16, 151–
    174
in Florida, 79–91
in Kansas, 93–121
in Michigan,
in New Mexico,
objectives of, 169–171
poverty-prone districts and, 63–66
race and, 63–66, 88–90, 104–106,
    112–114
size of district and, 63–66
summary of accomplishments,
    169–174
urban districts and, 63–66
Reform plans
California, 9–10, 11
Florida, 10, 11
Kansas, 10, 11
Michigan, 10
New Mexico, 10–11
Retirement fund, 97
Revenues (see also Per pupil revenues)
defined, 11n

measures, 26
nonfederal, 30
sources of, 1, 97
Revenue variables, 29–31
Rhode Island, 19*n*
Rodriguez v. *San Antonio [Texas]*
  Board of Education, 2*n*
Rolla (KS), 94*n*
Rural districts (*see* Urban vs. rural
  districts

Sales tax, 121
Senate Bill 90, 20, 41, 43
Serrano v. *Priest*, 2–3, 34, 167
Social Security fund, 31, 97
Sparsity factor, 139
Special education, 95, 96, 98, 124, 125,
  136, 139
"Squeeze factor," 43
State aid, 25, 50, 171–174
  Kansas, 94–95, 108, 116
  Michigan, 123–129 *passim*
  New Mexico, 139, 140–142
State Textbook Commission Fund, 80

Taxes, 26–27
  equity and, 1–2, 168–169
Tax neutrality
  in California, 52–55, 61–63, 70–72
    76
  in Florida, 83–89
  in Kansas, 102–104, 109–111, 117
  in Michigan, 129–131
  in New Mexico, 143–144
Tax rates, 166–167
  adjusted, 31
  California, 12, 52, 54, 56–59, 61, 69,
    70, 71–77
  distribution of, 157
  in Florida, 13, 83–85, 89, 90
  and foundation plans, 18–19
  in Kansas, 13–14, 96, 99–103,
    106–109, 114–116, 117, 119, 121
  in Michigan, 14, 124, 129, 131
  in New Mexico, 140–143
  reform and, 16, 151–154

regression on, 36
  as variable, 31
  wealth neutrality and, 62–63
Teachers, 26, 31, 52, 102, 148, 149, 156
  salaries and quality of, 21
Teachers' cost-adjustment provision,
  173–174
Tests, 22
Topeka (KS), 94*n*
Transportation costs, 79, 81, 94, 94*n*,
  95, 97, 98, 136, 139
Tuition, out-of-state, 136, 139

Unification bonus, 42, 43, 46
Unified school districts, California,
  66–75
Urban vs. rural districts
  in Florida, 88–90
  in Kansas, 104–106, 112–114,
    118–119
  in Michigan, 132, 133
  in New Mexico, 146, 148
  and reform, 63–66

Variable matching, defined, 10, 10*n*
Vocational education, 80, 95, 96, 97,
  98, 125, 139

Wealth
  defined, 28
  mean for adjusted, 36
  regression on adjusted, 36
Wealth neutrality, 35, 158–159
  in California, 12, 52–55, 61–63,
    70–72, 76
  in Florida, 83–89
  in Kansas, 102–104, 109–111, 117
  in Michigan, 14, 129–131, 133
  in New Mexico, 15, 143–144
  per pupil revenues and, 61–63
  reform and, 71, 72, 76
Weighting, 31–32
  in Florida, 80, 82
  formula, 23
Wichita (KS), 95
Workman's Compensation, 98

ABOUT THE AUTHORS

As deputy director of Rand's Institute for Civil Justice, **Stephen J. Carroll** is responsible for developing the Institute's research agenda, ensuring the quality and relevance of its projects, coordinating the staff, and overseeing the publication and dissemination of research results. Prior to joining the Institute, he had directed a series of research projects in the areas of human resources, education, and urban fiscal problems. A senior staff member of Rand's Economics Department since 1968, he has a B.S. degree in business administration (1962) and an M.S. in engineering economics (1964) from the Illinois Institute of Technology, and a Ph.D. in economics (1968) from Johns Hopkins University.

Rolla Edward Park is a senior economist at The Rand Corporation, with over fifteen years of experience in applied econometric analysis. He has concentrated on empirical research dealing with regulated and public industries, including air transportation, cable and broadcast television, education, the telephone industry, and electric power utilities. Before joining Rand, he worked as a civil engineer for the city of Los Angeles and Los Angeles International Airport. He holds a bachelor's degree in engineering from Caltech, a master's in business administration from UCLA, and a doctorate in economics from Princeton.